IT'S NOT YOU

WORKBOOK

AN ESSENTIAL GUIDE
TO RAMANI DURVASULA'S BOOK

OUR FREE GIFT TO YOU!

We wanted to take a moment to express our gratitude for your recent purchase from us. As a token of our appreciation, we are excited to offer you a complimentary set of our best-selling workbooks!

To claim your free workbooks, simply scan the QR code below with your smartphone or tablet, and follow the download instructions. These workbooks are packed with valuable tips and exercises to help you achieve your goals and maximize your productivity.

In addition to the GIFT, you'll also have access
to exclusive giveaways, discounts, and other valuable information.

NOTE FOR READERS

We would like to bring to your attention that we have created a summary and analysis workbook for the book titled "It's Not You". It is our intention to provide a valuable resource that complements your original reading experience, rather than serving as a replacement for it. Please note that this workbook has been meticulously crafted and is entirely free of plagiarism.

Our objective in producing this summary and analysis workbook is to provide you with an effective tool that can enhance your comprehension and involvement with the original material. However, we would like to emphasize that our summary and analysis workbook does not substitute for the original source material.

TABLE OF CONTENTS

WORKBOOK OVERVIEW...06

INTRODUCTION...08

HOW TO USE IT..10

YOUR JOURNEY..12

PART I: THE NARCISSISTIC RELATIONSHIP...14

CHAPTER 1. CLARIFYING NARCISSISM...14

CHAPTER 2. DEATH BY A THOUSAND CUTS: THE NARCISSISTIC RELATIONSHIP............26

CHAPTER 3. THE FALLOUT: THE IMPACT OF NARCISSISTIC ABUSE......................38

PART II: RECOGNITION, RECOVERY, HEALING, AND GROWTH........................48

CHAPTER 4. UNDERSTAND YOUR BACKSTORY...48

CHAPTER 5. EMBRACE RADICAL ACCEPTANCE.......................................60

CHAPTER 6. GRIEF AND HEALING FROM NARCISSISTIC RELATIONSHIPS..........70

CHAPTER 7. BECOME MORE NARCISSIST RESISTANT..............................80

CHAPTER 8. HEAL AND GROW WHEN YOU STAY......................................92

CHAPTER 9. REWRITE YOUR STORY...102

WORKBOOK OVERVIEW

In the introduction of this workbook, we'll guide you through an overview of "It's Not You: Identifying and Healing from Narcissistic People" by Ramani Durvasula and provide insights on how to effectively use this workbook alongside the main text. This companion workbook is designed to be a valuable resource for your personal journey of understanding and healing from narcissistic relationships.

Reflective Journey

Start by reflecting on your own experiences and emotions surrounding narcissistic individuals. Engage in exercises that delve into your past relationships, identifying patterns of behavior and the impact they have had on your sense of self-worth and well-being. By exploring your own journey, you'll lay the foundation for understanding and healing from narcissistic abuse.

Connection and Communication

Delve into the complexities of communication within narcissistic relationships. Explore the tactics commonly used by narcissists to manipulate and control their victims and learn how to recognize and respond to these behaviors effectively. Develop strategies for setting boundaries and asserting your needs in interactions with narcissistic individuals, fostering healthier communication patterns.

Understanding Struggles and Strengths

Investigate the psychological dynamics at play in narcissistic relationships, including the narcissist's underlying insecurities and motivations. Reflect on your own vulnerabilities and strengths, recognizing how they may influence your interactions with narcissistic individuals. Explore methods for cultivating self-compassion and resilience in the face of narcissistic abuse, empowering yourself to break free from toxic patterns.

Holistic Exploration

The workbook takes you on a holistic exploration of narcissism, addressing its impact on various aspects of your life including relationships, self-esteem, and emotional well-being. Engage in activities that promote self-discovery and personal growth, fostering a deeper understanding of yourself and your experiences with narcissisti individuals. By examining narcissism from multiple perspectives, you'll gain insights that facilitate healing and transformation.

Application to Real Life

Tailored exercises and reflection questions are provided to help you apply the concepts of "It's Not You" to your own life. Whether setting boundaries with a narcissistic family member, navigating a toxic work environment, or rebuilding your self-esteem after narcissistic abuse, this workbook serves as a practical guide for real-world application. By integrating the insights gained from the main text into your daily interactions and decision-making, you'll empower yourself to create positive change and cultivate healthier relationships.

Empowerment for Healing

This workbook is crafted to empower you on your journey of healing and recovery from narcissistic relationships. By engaging with the content of "It's Not You" through introspective exercises and practical tools, you'll develop the resilience and self-awareness needed to break free from the cycle of abuse and reclaim your sense of self. Through reflection, exploration, and action, you'll emerge stronger and more empowered to create a life free from the toxic influence of narcissistic individuals.

INTRODUCTION

OVERVIEW OF "IT'S NOT YOU"

"Identifying and Healing from Narcissistic People"

In a world where narcissistic individuals wield their charm like a double-edged sword, leaving behind a trail of emotional devastation, Dr. Ramani Durvasula offers a beacon of hope and healing. With her unparalleled expertise as a clinical psychologist specializing in narcissistic relationships, Dr. Durvasula presents a transformative guide to protecting oneself from the daily harms of narcissism in her groundbreaking book, "It's Not You."

Through her work spanning over two decades, Dr. Durvasula has delved deep into the intricate landscape of narcissism, unraveling its nuances and equipping survivors with the tools they need to reclaim their lives. In "It's Not You," she elucidates how narcissists ensnare their victims with charisma one moment and inflict emotional turmoil the next, leaving behind a lingering sense of self-doubt and confusion.

With compassion and clarity, Dr. Durvasula dismantles the myth that victims of narcissistic abuse are somehow responsible for their torment. Instead, she empowers readers to recognize the insidious tactics of narcissists and reclaim their agency in the healing process. Drawing upon her wealth of experience and research, she decodes the behavioral patterns that signify narcissistic behavior, enabling readers to navigate the tumultuous waters of these toxic relationships with newfound resilience.

"It's Not You" is more than just a survival guide; it is a roadmap to liberation and self-discovery. Dr. Durvasula offers practical strategies for becoming gaslight-resistant, breaking free from trauma bonds, and establishing healthy boundaries. Through poignant anecdotes and actionable insights, she guides readers on a journey of healing, inviting them to release the burden of blame and embrace their authentic selves.

In a world where narcissism runs rampant, "It's Not You" serves as a beacon of hope, illuminating the path toward healing and empowerment. Dr. Ramani Durvasula compassionate wisdom and unwavering commitment to truth make this book an indispensable companion for anyone seeking to break free from the grip of narcissistic abuse and reclaim their sense of self-worth.

ABOUT THE AUTHOR

Dr. Ramani Durvasula is a licensed clinical psychologist in Los Angeles, CA, Professor Emerita of Psychology at California State University, Los Angeles, and the Founder and CEO of LUNA Education, Training & Consulting.

She is the author of several books including "It's Not You: Identifying and Healing from Narcissistic People" and "Should I Stay or Should I Go: Surviving A Relationship with a Narcissist", and "Don't You Know Who I Am?: How to Stay Sane in an Era of Narcissism, Entitlement, and Incivility". The focus of Dr. Durvasula's clinical, academic, and consultative work is the etiology and impact of narcissism and high-conflict, entitled, antagonistic personality styles on human relationships, mental health, and societal expectations.

Her work has been featured at SXSW, TEDx, Red Table Talk, the Today Show, and Investigation Discovery. You can also find her on YouTube where she has accumulated millions of views on her videos discussing narcissism on her successful channel, and on social media @DoctorRamani. Now she will be adding the role of host to her resume as she launches her new podcast, Navigating Narcissism with Dr. Ramani, a show that focuses on narcissism and its impact on relationships.

HOW TO USE IT

Welcome to the workbook companion for "It's Not You: Identifying and Healing from Narcissistic People" by Ramani Durvasula. This workbook is designed to enhance your exploration of the book and support you in applying its insights to your journey of healing and empowerment. Here's a guide on how to make the most of this resource

Read the Book First
Begin by thoroughly reading "It's Not You" by Ramani Durvasula. Familiarize yourself with the concepts, stories, and strategies presented in the main text. This foundational understanding will serve as a springboard for your engagement with the workbook.

Set Clear Objectives
Take some time to clarify your objectives for using this workbook. Are you seeking to recognize narcissistic behavior in your relationships, establish healthier boundaries or heal from past narcissistic abuse? Clearly defining your goals will help you focus your efforts and derive maximum benefit from the workbook.

Correspondence with Chapters
Align each section of the workbook with the relevant chapters in the main book. This alignment ensures that you can seamlessly apply the principles and exercises from each chapter to your own experiences and reflections.

Reflect and Document
Engage thoughtfully with the workbook's questions and exercises designed to prompt reflection. Use the provided space to document your thoughts, feelings, and insights as you work through each section. Writing down your responses will help you internalize the concepts and track your progress over time.

Actionable Steps
Translate your reflections into actionable steps. Identify specific strategies and behaviors you can implement to protect yourself from narcissistic abuse, strengthen your boundaries, and cultivate healthier relationships. Set clear goals and timeline for implementing these changes in your life.

Track Your Growth

Utilize the tracking space in the workbook to monitor your progress. Record any positive shifts in your understanding of narcissism, your ability to set boundaries, or your overall well-being. Regularly revisiting your tracked progress will reinforce your commitment to personal growth.

Seek Support and Dialogue

If you encounter challenges or have questions during your journey, don't hesitate to seek support. Engage in dialogues with trusted friends, family members, or support groups to share experiences and gain insights. Collaborating with others can provide valuable perspective and encouragement.

Consistent Commitment

Understand that healing from narcissistic abuse is a journey that requires consistent commitment. Stay patient and compassionate with yourself as you navigate this process. Regularly revisit the workbook to review your progress, refine your strategies, and celebrate your achievements.

By following these steps and using this workbook as a tool for self-reflection and growth, you'll amplify the impact of "It's Not You" in your journey toward healing and empowerment. Here's to reclaiming your sense of self and fostering healthier relationships!

YOUR JOURNEY

Intentionally left blank for your reflections, use this space to jot down goals, intentions, and past experiences. Compare your growth by the end. Embrace vulnerability and the journey. We hope this workbook aids you towards the better.

PART I: THE NARCISSISTIC RELATIONSHIP

CHAPTER 1: CLARIFYING NARCISSISM

Summary

Narcissism, often misunderstood and pervasive in contemporary society, presents itself in various forms, challenging our perceptions of empathy, self-centeredness, and interpersonal dynamics. Jonathan Franzen's assertion, "The personality susceptible to the dream of limitless freedom is a personality also prone, should the dream ever sour, to misanthropy and rage," encapsulates the complexities surrounding narcissism. Through the narratives of Carlos and Joanna, the author delves into the intricate layers of narcissistic behavior and its impact on relationships.

In exploring the lives of Carlos and Joanna, the author sheds light on the subtle manifestations of narcissism within personal relationships. Portrayed as empathetic yet flawed, Carlos grapples with moments of indiscretion while maintaining genuine care for those around him. Despite his altruistic tendencies, Carlos's lapses in judgment underscore the vulnerability inherent in human relationships, where the line between empathy and self-interest blurs. Joanna's experiences with Adam provide a stark contrast, revealing a more insidious side of narcissism characterized by manipulation and emotional neglect. Adam's oscillation between grand gestures and emotional withdrawal reflects the tumultuous nature of narcissistic dynamics, leaving Joanna torn between loyalty and self-preservation.

Understanding Narcissism: Debunking Myths
Narcissism defies simplistic definitions, transcending mere self-involvement to encompass a spectrum of behaviors and traits. The author challenges the prevailing

misconceptions, illustrating how narcissism permeates various facets of life, from romantic entanglements to professional dynamics. By unraveling the nuances of narcissistic behavior, we confront the pervasive yet elusive nature of this personality disorder. Through introspection and critical analysis, we dismantle stereotypes and embrace the complexity of human interactions shaped by narcissistic tendencies.

Central to narcissism are multifaceted traits that shape interactions and perceptions. From the insatiable need for validation, or "narcissistic supply," to the delusional grandiosity that underpins self-perception, each feature contributes to a complex portrait of narcissistic individuals. Egocentricity, inconsistency, and entitlement emerge as hallmarks of narcissistic behavior, perpetuating cycles of manipulation and emotional turmoil. By dissecting these traits, we gain insight into the underlying insecurities driving narcissistic tendencies and the mechanisms through which individuals navigate relationships and assert dominance.

Navigating Narcissistic Relationships

The dynamic nature of narcissism complicates interpersonal dynamics, veering between charm and aggression with unsettling unpredictability. As victims of narcissistic abuse grapple with guilt and self-doubt, the author underscores the insidious nature of entitlement and insecurity underlying narcissistic behavior. By illuminating the mechanisms through which narcissism operates, we gain insight into its far-reaching implications on personal well-being and societal norms. Through empathy and self-reflection, we navigate the complexities of narcissistic relationships, fostering dialogue and understanding to pave the path toward healthier interactions and collective healing from the wounds of narcissistic abuse.

Being Thin-skinned

The author illustrates how narcissistic individuals struggle with receiving criticism or feedback, often reacting with disproportionate rage and defensiveness. Despite projecting an image of confidence, they harbor a chronic need for reassurance, albeit unwilling to explicitly seek it. An anecdote featuring a woman obsessed with appearances highlights the delicate balance of offering ease without triggering feelings of vulnerability and shame. This dance of narcissistic reactive sensitivity, coupled with a perpetual sense of victimhood, underscores the inherent challenges of navigating relationships with such individuals.

Inability to self-regulate

Narcissistic individuals exhibit a profound inability to manage their emotions, stemming from a deep-seated fear of vulnerability and shame. Their reactive outbursts and blame-shifting serve as mechanisms to preserve their grandiose facade and assert dominance. Lacking genuine empathy, they struggle to comprehend the emotional impact of their actions on others, offering hollow apologies to alleviate interpersonal conflicts. The author emphasizes the intricate interplay between shame, rage, and emotional regulation within the narcissistic psyche.

Need for Dominance

Motivated by a relentless pursuit of dominance and control, narcissistic individuals prioritize power dynamics over genuine intimacy and connection. Their relationships become transactional arrangements; others serve as mere conduits for their gratification and validation. The author juxtaposes the narcissistic quest for superiority with the relational values of empathy and reciprocity, highlighting the fundamental disconnect underlying narcissistic dynamics.

Lack of Empathy

While possessing cognitive empathy, narcissistic individuals exhibit a superficial and inconsistent capacity for understanding and responding to the emotions of others. Their heart serves as a strategic tool for manipulation rather than genuine compassion, fluctuating in tandem with their need for validation and supply. The author illustrates this dynamic through contrasting scenarios of empathic engagement and callous indifference, underscoring the transactional nature of narcissistic relationships.

Contempt for Others

Narcissistic individuals harbor a deep-seated contempt for the vulnerabilities and needs of others, viewing dependency as a threat to their perceived superiority. Their disdain often manifests as passive-aggressive behavior, a defense mechanism against confronting their insecurities. The author explores the paradox of narcissistic contempt, wherein the perceived weaknesses of others serve as mirrors reflecting their internal fragility.

Projection of Shame

Projection emerges as a common defense mechanism among narcissistic individuals enabling them to displace their shameful attributes onto others. This psychological maneuver shields their fragile self-image from the discomfort of introspection perpetuating cycles of blame and manipulation. Through anecdotes of projection in interpersonal dynamics, the author elucidates the insidious nature of narcissistic projection and its impact on relational trust and authenticity.

Despite exhibiting toxic behaviors, narcissistic individuals often exude charm confidence, and intelligence, luring others into their orbit through charismatic personas. The author underscores the discrepancy between surface-level allure and underlying manipulative tendencies, cautioning against conflating narcissism with genuine success or ambition. By unmasking the facade of charm, the author invites readers to discern the subtle red flags of narcissistic behavior.

The Continuum of Narcissism

Narcissism exists along a continuum, ranging from superficial displays of self absorption to severe manifestations of exploitation and violence. Through the narrative of Marcus and Melissa, the author delineates the complexities of moderate narcissism, characterized by cognitive empathy and entitlement. The author highlights the duplicitous nature of moderate narcissists, who oscillate between composed public personas and volatile private behaviors, leaving victims bewildered and isolated.

The Different Types of Narcissism:

1. <u>Grandiose:</u> Grandiose narcissism epitomizes the classical depiction of narcissistic personality traits characterized by charm, grandiosity, and attention-seeking behavior. The author underscores the allure of grandiose narcissists, whose charisma and ambition often overshadow their toxic tendencies. However, beneath the veneer of success lies a fragile ego, prone to volatility and projection. Through nuanced exploration, the author challenges prevailing perceptions of narcissism, urging readers to discern the subtle manifestations of this complex personality disorder.

2. <u>Vulnerable Narcissism:</u> The author delves into the intricacies of vulnerable narcissism, a subtype characterized by a sense of victimization and covert behaviors. Through introspection, individuals exhibiting vulnerable narcissism often perceive themselves as unrecognized geniuses, attributing their lack of success to external factors. Their malcontented nature fuels oppositional behavior and chronic dissatisfaction, manifesting in arguments and resistance to engagement. Despite outward appearances of low self-esteem, vulnerable narcissists harbor a grandiose sense of entitlement and an aversion to accountability, perpetuating cycles of resentment and emotional volatility. Their struggles with abandonment and rejection sensitivity compound the complexity of their interpersonal relationships, creating a constant state of emotional turmoil.

3. <u>Communal Narcissism:</u> The author explores communal narcissism, a distinct subtype characterized by a collective pursuit of validation and admiration. Unlike traditional narcissists who prioritize self-aggrandizement, communal narcissists derive validation from altruistic endeavors, positioning themselves as paragons of selflessness and virtue. Whether through charitable acts or public displays of generosity, communal narcissists cultivate a saintly image while demanding recognition and praise. Their involvement in community-centric settings further reinforces their grandiose identity, masking underlying patterns of manipulation and control. The author underscores the pervasive nature of communal narcissism, which often manifests in familial dynamics marked by disinterest and emotional neglect.

4. <u>Self-righteous Narcissism:</u> In examining self-righteous narcissism, the author illuminates a rigid, judgmental worldview characterized by moral superiority and disdain for deviation from prescribed norms. Self-righteous narcissists maintain an unwavering belief in their infallibility, dismissing alternative perspectives as inferior and unworthy of consideration. Their adherence to strict routines and disdain for emotional expression reflect a profound aversion to vulnerability,

perpetuating cycles of isolation and interpersonal conflict. By imposing their values onto others, self-righteous narcissists foster an environment of control and manipulation devoid of empathy and genuine human connection.

5. Neglectful Narcissism: Neglectful narcissism, as elucidated by the author, epitomizes detachment and emotional disengagement within interpersonal relationships. Individuals exhibiting neglectful narcissism display a profound lack of empathy and interest in others, relegating relationships to superficial interactions devoid of genuine connection. Their disregard for emotional needs and autonomy creates an atmosphere of emotional abandonment, leaving partners and loved ones feeling invisible and invalidated. The author emphasizes the profound impact of neglectful narcissism on relational dynamics, where individuals are left to navigate emotional voids and existential isolation.

6. Malignant Narcissism: The author delves into the darkest manifestations of narcissism with malignant narcissism, characterized by a toxic blend of narcissistic, psychopathic, and sadistic tendencies. Malignant narcissists wield power and manipulation to exert control over others, deriving pleasure from inflicting emotional harm and instilling fear. Their vindictive nature and propensity for aggression create an atmosphere of intimidation and coercion, leaving victims traumatized and emotionally scarred. The author underscores the insidious nature of malignant narcissism, where individuals prioritize dominance and self-preservation at the expense of human dignity and well-being.

Navigating Narcissism vs. Narcissistic Personality Disorder
The author navigates the complexities of distinguishing narcissism from narcissistic personality disorder (NPD), highlighting the nuanced interplay between personality styles and clinical diagnoses. While narcissism encompasses a broad spectrum of traits and behaviors, NPD represents a clinical manifestation characterized by pervasive impairment and distress. The author challenges prevailing stigmas surrounding NPD, advocating for a nuanced understanding of narcissistic behaviors and their impact on interpersonal relationships. By demystifying misconceptions and fostering empathy, the author empowers individuals to navigate narcissistic dynamics with clarity and self-assurance, promoting resilience and healing in the face of adversity.

Myths about Narcissism
We miss something important when we try to simplify narcissism or boil it down to one trait. The author addresses prevailing myths about narcissism, shedding light on its multifaceted nature and the complexities it introduces into personal interactions. Narcissism encompasses a range of behaviors and attitudes beyond mere arrogance or self-centeredness. By exploring these misconceptions, we gain a deeper understanding of how narcissism operates and its impact on relationships

Narcissistic People Are Always Men

Contrary to popular belief, narcissism transcends gender boundaries. While grandiose narcissism is more prevalent among men, instances of narcissism can be found across all genders. The author challenges stereotypes and emphasizes recognizing toxic patterns irrespective of gender. By acknowledging the diverse manifestations of narcissism, we dismantle harmful stereotypes and foster a more inclusive understanding of this complex personality trait.

It's Just Bragging and Arrogance

Arrogance is merely the tip of the iceberg when it comes to narcissistic behavior. The author distinguishes between arrogance and narcissism, highlighting the latter's deeper psychological roots in insecurity and fragility. By delving into the nuances of narcissistic behavior, we gain insight into its profound impact on interpersonal dynamics. Understanding the underlying motivations behind narcissistic tendencies is crucial in addressing their harmful effects on relationships and personal well-being.

They Can't Control Their Behavior

Narcissistic individuals possess a remarkable ability to manipulate their behavior based on social context. The author illustrates how narcissists strategically manage their interactions, projecting charm in public while unleashing their aggression in private. This dichotomy underscores the calculated nature of selfish behavior and its profound effects on personal relationships. By examining the mechanisms of behavioral control within narcissistic individuals, we confront the complexities of navigating relationships with them and assert boundaries to protect ourselves.

Narcissists Can Significantly Change

The prospect of change within narcissistic individuals is slim, rooted in the inherent stability of personality traits. Despite popular narratives of redemption, the author emphasizes the arduous nature of personality transformation and the limited research supporting significant behavioral change in narcissistic individuals. By acknowledging the challenges of change, we temper unrealistic expectations and focus on understanding and managing narcissistic behaviors within relationships.

Mental Health Issues That Overlap with Narcissism

Narcissism often overlaps with various mental health issues, complicating diagnosis and treatment. From ADHD to addiction, the author explores the intricate connections between narcissism and co-occurring disorders. Understanding these overlaps is crucial in navigating relationships with narcissistic individuals and seeking appropriate support. By recognizing the interplay between narcissism and other mental health conditions, we address the complexity of treatment and support systems for individuals struggling with narcissistic tendencies.

In conclusion, understanding narcissism demands a nuanced perspective, transcending simplistic stereotypes. The author confronts the intricate interplay of behaviors and traits by debunking myths and exploring their varied manifestations. Carlos and Adam's narratives highlight the diverse spectrum of narcissistic behavior, urging us to navigate relationships with empathy and clarity. Recognizing the cycle of narcissistic abuse is pivotal for fostering healing and self-discovery. By reframing guilt and promoting empathy, we empower ourselves to forge healthier interactions and prioritize emotional well-being. Embracing the complexities of narcissism, we embark on a journey of resilience and collective growth, fostering dialogue and understanding along the way.

LESSONS AND KEY POINTS FROM THIS CHAPTER

1. The author unravels the complexities of narcissism through the narratives of Carlos and Joanna, highlighting the subtle manifestations within personal relationships.

2. Understanding narcissism involves debunking myths and embracing its multifaceted nature, transcending simplistic definitions and stereotypes perpetuated by societal norms.

3. Narcissistic traits, from entitlement to manipulation, shape interpersonal dynamics, underscoring the need for discernment and boundary-setting in relationships with narcissistic individuals.

4. Navigating narcissistic relationships requires empathy and self-reflection empowering individuals to confront the insidious nature of entitlement and emotional manipulation.

5. Narcissistic individuals exhibit thin-skinned reactions to criticism, projecting a facade of confidence while harbouring deep-seated insecurities and emotional fragility.

6. The author delves into the inability of narcissists to self-regulate, highlighting their propensity for reactive outbursts and blame-shifting to preserve their grandiose self-image.

7. Motivated by a relentless need for dominance, narcissistic individuals prioritize power dynamics over genuine intimacy, perpetuating cycles of manipulation and emotional turmoil.

8. Despite possessing cognitive empathy, narcissists lack genuine compassion and exhibit superficial empathy as a tool for manipulation rather than sincere understanding.

9. Narcissistic contempt for others reflects their deep-seated disdain for vulnerability and dependency, perpetuating passive-aggressive behaviours and emotional detachment.

10. The author navigates the continuum of narcissism, ranging from grandiose to malignant manifestations, highlighting the nuanced interplay between personality styles and clinical diagnoses.

REFLECTION QUESTIONS

These questions can help guide your reflection on the chapter and facilitate a deeper understanding of the author's message and ideas.

How do you perceive the balance between giving and receiving in your relationships? Do you feel valued and appreciated, or do you often give more than you receive?

Reflecting on past experiences, have you ever felt misunderstood or invalidated by someone close to you? How did it make you think, and how did you navigate through those emotions?

Think about when you had to confront criticism or feedback from others. How did you react, and could you separate the feedback from your sense of self-worth?

Consider your interactions with others. Do you often seek validation or approval from external sources, or do you feel comfortable and confident in your skin?

Reflect on moments of conflict or disagreement in your relationships. How do you typically handle disagreements, and can you maintain open communication and empathy towards others?

MILESTONE GOALS

1. Readers need to recognize subtle signs of narcissism in personal relationships, fostering healthier boundaries and discernment in interactions to mitigate potential emotional manipulation and abuse.

2. Another goal is understanding the intricate dynamics of narcissistic behaviour equipping readers with insights to navigate complex interpersonal relationships with empathy and clarity.

3. Readers should aim to cultivate self-awareness and resilience in the face o narcissistic abuse, prioritizing emotional well-being and seeking support to break free from toxic patterns and foster healing.

ACTIONABLE MOVEMENTS

1. **Reflect on personal interactions:** Take time to assess past interactions and identify any patterns of narcissistic behavior, both in yourself and others.

2. **Educate yourself:** Dive deeper into resources about narcissism to gain a better understanding of its nuances and how it manifests in various contexts.

3. **Set boundaries:** Establish boundaries in relationships to protect your emotional well-being and prevent manipulation or abuse.

4. **Seek support:** Reach out to trusted friends, family members, or mental health professionals for guidance and support in navigating relationships affected by narcissism.

5. **Practice empathy:** Cultivate empathy towards individuals exhibiting narcissistic tendencies while maintaining awareness of the need to prioritize self-care.

6. **Foster open communication:** Encourage open and honest communication in relationships, fostering an environment where concerns can be addressed constructively.

7. **Prioritize self-reflection:** Engage in regular self-reflection to identify any potential narcissistic traits within yourself and work towards personal growth and development.

8. **Challenge societal norms:** Challenge societal norms that perpetuate harmful stereotypes about gender and narcissism, advocating for greater awareness and understanding.

9. **Advocate for mental health resources:** Advocate for increased access to mental health resources and support systems for individuals affected by narcissism and other related disorders.

10. **Lead by example:** Lead by example in promoting healthy relationship dynamics and emotional intelligence, inspiring others to prioritize empathy and understanding in their interactions.

In the empty pages ahead, you can explore this chapter more deeply and make it your own. Take this opportunity to write your thoughts, ideas, and questions about what you've read so far. Feel free to brainstorm, draw, or note down any questions that pop into your head.

CHAPTER 2:
DEATH BY A THOUSAND CUTS:
THE NARCISSISTIC RELATIONSHIP

Summary

In this chapter, the author paints a vivid portrait of Jordan's turbulent journey through the tumultuous waters of familial narcissism. Jordan's struggle to reconcile his longing for paternal approval with the harsh reality of his father's narcissistic behavior serves as a poignant exploration of the complexities inherent in such relationships. Through Jordan's narrative, readers are invited to delve into the intricate dynamics of narcissistic abuse and its profound impact on personal identity and emotional well-being.

Jordan emerges as a compelling protagonist whose experiences resonate with the universal themes of longing, rejection, and the search for validation. From his childhood spent yearning for his father's affection to his adult struggles with identity and self-worth, Jordan's story epitomizes the profound influence of narcissistic abuse on individual development and interpersonal relationships. Through Jordan's lens, the author skillfully navigates the intricate nuances of narcissistic dynamics, offering readers a window into the complexities of familial dysfunction and emotional trauma.

Understanding Narcissistic Abuse

Narcissistic abuse emerges as a pervasive and insidious phenomenon that permeates every facet of victims' lives. Drawing upon extensive research and clinical expertise, the author elucidates the multifaceted nature of narcissistic abuse, exploring its far-reaching implications for victims' psychological well-being and interpersonal relationships. By unpacking the underlying dynamics of narcissistic behavior, the narrative sheds light on the power dynamics at play within abusive relationships and the profound toll they exact on victims' sense of self and agency.

Exploring Narcissistic Traits

The author underscores the heterogeneity of narcissistic abuse, emphasizing its varied manifestations along a continuum of severity and intensity. From subtle forms of emotional manipulation to overt acts of coercion and control, narcissistic abuse encompasses a diverse array of behaviors that erode victims' autonomy and self-esteem. Through Jordan's narrative, readers gain insight into the nuanced interplay between public facades and private realities, illuminating the stark dissonance between outward appearances of normalcy and the hidden depths of emotional turmoil and despair.

Gaslighting emerges as a central theme in the narrative, serving as a potent tool of manipulation and control wielded by narcissistic abusers. Through a systematic campaign of doubt and distortion, gaslighters undermine victims' perceptions of reality, fostering a sense of confusion and disorientation. The author skillfully unpacks the mechanics of gaslighting, illuminating its insidious impact on victims' mental health and emotional well-being. By elucidating the subtle tactics employed by gaslighters, the narrative empowers readers to recognize and confront the pervasive influence of narcissistic abuse within their own lives and relationships.

The author offers readers a roadmap for identifying the telltale signs of gaslighting, from subtle denial and deflection to overt attempts at emotional manipulation. By arming readers with the tools to discern manipulation from genuine interaction, the narrative enables individuals to reclaim agency and autonomy within their relationships. Through the exploration of gaslighting dynamics, readers are challenged to confront the pervasive influence of narcissistic abuse and its enduring impact on personal identity and emotional well-being. In shedding light on the complexities of narcissistic behavior, the narrative empowers readers to break free from the cycle of manipulation and reclaim their sense of self.

The DIMMER Patterns

The author delves into the intricate dynamics of narcissistic abuse through the lens of specific behavioral patterns encapsulated by DIMMER. This acronym serves as a poignant metaphor for the gradual dimming of one's sense of self and well-being within narcissistic relationships. Dismissiveness, invalidation, minimization, manipulation, exploitativeness, and rage are illuminated as pervasive mechanisms through which narcissistic individuals exert dominance and control. These patterns, ranging from subtle dismissals to overt displays of anger, collectively erode victims' autonomy and sense of worth, perpetuating a cycle of emotional turmoil and despair.

Dismissiveness and Invalidation

Jordan's story exemplifies the profound impact of dismissiveness and invalidation within narcissistic relationships. From his father's contemptuous disregard for his achievements to his mother's silent acquiescence to paternal tyranny, Jordan's narrative underscores the dehumanizing effects of chronic dismissal and negation.

The author poignantly illustrates how invalidation gradually erodes victims' sense of self, leaving them feeling unheard, unseen, and ultimately invisible in the eyes of their abuser.

Minimization and Manipulation

The author highlights the insidious nature of minimization and manipulation as tools of narcissistic control. Through subtle acts of downplaying and trivializing victims' experiences, narcissistic individuals undermine their sense of significance and self-worth. Manipulation, meanwhile, operates as a means of exploiting victims' vulnerabilities to serve the narcissist's agenda. Jordan's futile attempts to garner his father's approval through conformity and compromise serve as a poignant reminder of the manipulative dynamics inherent in narcissistic relationships.

Exploitativeness and Rage

Exploitativeness emerges as a defining feature of narcissistic abuse, characterized by the narcissist's relentless pursuit of self-interest at the expense of others. Jordan's father's unrelenting demands for attention and admiration epitomize the exploitative nature of narcissistic relationships, wherein victims are coerced into fulfilling the narcissist's insatiable need for validation. Meanwhile, the author delves into the chilling manifestations of narcissistic rage, which serve as a potent mechanism of control and intimidation within abusive dynamics, leaving victims trapped in a cycle of fear and subservience.

The Domination Patterns

The author delves into the pervasive dynamics of domination, isolation, revenge, and threats within narcissistic relationships. These patterns serve as instruments of control through which narcissistic individuals assert their dominance and superiority over their victims. From coercive control tactics to vindictive acts of retaliation, narcissistic abuse manifests in various forms of psychological and emotional manipulation designed to subjugate and disempower victims.

Coercive Control and Isolation

The author elucidates how narcissistic individuals leverage tactics of coercion and isolation to maintain dominance over their victims. Jordan's narrative illustrates how narcissistic abusers systematically undermine their victims' support networks fostering a sense of dependency and vulnerability. By criticizing and disparaging victims' relationships and achievements, narcissists isolate their victims, rendering them increasingly reliant on the abuser for validation and validation.

Revenge and Threats

Revenge and threats emerge as potent tools of manipulation and intimidation within narcissistic relationships. Jordan's father's vindictive behavior and propensity for retaliation underscore the lengths to which narcissistic individuals will go to maintain control over their victims. Through threats of legal action, financial coercion, and emotional blackmail, narcissists instill a pervasive sense of fear and insecurity in their victims, perpetuating a cycle of dominance and subservience.

The Disagreeable Patterns

The author explores the discordant dynamics of arguing, blame-shifting, and word salad within narcissistic relationships. These patterns serve as mechanisms through which narcissistic individuals seek to control the narrative and assert their superiority over their victims. From engaging in endless debates to employing tactics of manipulation and gaslighting, narcissists systematically undermine their victims' sense of agency and self-worth, perpetuating a cycle of confusion and despair.

Arguing and Baiting

The author highlights the role of arguing and baiting as tactics of manipulation and control within narcissistic relationships. Through incessant conflicts and provocations, narcissistic individuals undermine their victims' emotional well-being, leaving them feeling drained and powerless. Jordan's futile attempts to reason with his father serve as a poignant reminder of the futility of engaging in conflict with narcissistic abusers, who thrive on discord and chaos to maintain their dominance.

Blame-Shifting and Rationalization

Blame-shifting and rationalization emerge as pervasive patterns within narcissistic relationships, serving as mechanisms through which narcissistic individuals evade accountability and perpetuate their sense of superiority. Jordan's mother's complicity in his father's abusive behavior exemplifies the insidious nature of blame-shifting, wherein victims are gaslit into believing they are responsible for their suffering. By justifying and rationalizing their actions, narcissists further erode their victims' sense of reality, perpetuating a cycle of self-doubt and confusion.

Criticism and Humiliation

Criticism and humiliation serve as weapons of emotional manipulation within narcissistic relationships, wherein victims are systematically degraded and devalued to bolster the narcissist's sense of superiority. Jordan's experiences of ridicule and contempt at the hands of his father underscore the profound impact of emotional abuse on victims' self-esteem and well-being. By subjecting their victims to constant scrutiny and scorn, narcissists instill a pervasive sense of shame and inadequacy, perpetuating a cycle of emotional turmoil and despair.

The Narcissistic Relationship Cycle

The author delves into the cyclical nature of narcissistic relationships through the story of Asha and Dave. Dave's charm and attentiveness initially captivated Asha, which gradually gave way to periods of resentment and entitlement. As Dave oscillates between moments of affection and anger, Asha finds herself walking on eggshells, striving to meet his shifting expectations. Despite her growing disillusionment, Asha remains hopeful that Dave will change, only to be trapped in a relentless cycle of idealization and devaluation.

Understanding Narcissistic Abuse

The author highlights the universal patterns of narcissistic abuse, which often begin with love bombing and culminate in devaluation and discard. Drawing parallels between Asha's experience and broader relational dynamics, the author underscores the pervasive influence of narcissistic behavior on victims' sense of self-worth and agency. By elucidating the underlying mechanisms of abuse, the narrative empowers readers to recognize and confront the insidious nature of narcissistic relationships in their own lives.

Tactics of Narcissistic Abuse

Gaslighting emerges as a central theme in the narrative, with Dave employing manipulation and denial to undermine Asha's perceptions of reality. Through the lens of gaslighting dynamics, the author explores the power imbalances inherent in narcissistic relationships, shedding light on the subtle tactics used to erode victims' autonomy and self-esteem. By unraveling the intricacies of gaslighting, the narrative equips readers with the tools to identify and challenge the coercive tactics employed by narcissistic abusers.

The Love Bomb: The False Fairy Tale

The author delves into the phenomenon of love bombing, tracing its insidious role in drawing victims into narcissistic relationships. Through Asha's journey, readers are invited to explore the seductive allure of love bombing and its role in fostering dependency and manipulation. By examining the psychological underpinnings of love bombing, the narrative prompts readers to interrogate their vulnerabilities and expectations within the context of romantic relationships.

Devaluation: The Unfolding of Narcissistic Abuse

The transition from love bombing to devaluation marks a critical turning point in narcissistic relationships, as the idealized facade gives way to resentment and contempt. Through Asha's narrative, the author elucidates the emotional toll of devaluation, highlighting the profound sense of confusion and betrayal experienced by victims. By unpacking the cyclical nature of narcissistic abuse, the narrative offers insight into the complexities of relational dynamics and the enduring impact of emotional manipulation.

Discard: "This Isn't Working for Me Anymore . . ."

The author illustrates the discard phase as a pivotal juncture in narcissistic relationships where one party, whether the narcissist or the victim, signals the end of the relationship. Discarding doesn't always result in the termination of the relationship but signifies a depletion of emotional connection and investment. Jordan's experiences with his father's dismissive behaviors resonate with the patterns observed during the discard phase. This phase often witnesses escalated abuse, intensified gaslighting, and unmasked contempt as the narcissistic individual seeks to maintain control and dominance.

Hoovering: "Hey, I've Been Thinking of You. Let's Give It a Fresh Start."

The author delves into the phenomenon of hoovering, wherein narcissistic individuals attempt to re-engage former partners or victims, drawing them back into the relationship dynamic. Through Jordan's narrative, readers gain insight into the seductive allure of hoovering, characterized by promises of change, pseudo-apologies, and manipulative tactics. Hoovering epitomizes the cyclical nature of narcissistic relationships, wherein victims are lured back into a familiar yet toxic dynamic despite their better judgment.

Trauma Bonds: The Riptide of the Narcissistic Relationship

The author explores the concept of trauma bonds as pervasive emotional ties that bind victims to their narcissistic abusers. Through Asha's story, readers confront the complexities of trauma bonding, which transcend conventional notions of dependency or addiction. Trauma bonds manifest as a deep-seated sense of love and connection that obscures victims' perceptions of abuse and manipulation. By shedding light on the insidious nature of trauma bonds, the author empowers readers to recognize and break free from the riptide of narcissistic relationships.

The harm inflicted by narcissistic abuse transcends the realm of individual pathology, permeating interpersonal dynamics and leaving indelible scars on victims' psyches. Through compelling narratives and insightful analysis, the author elucidates the pervasive impact of narcissistic behavior on victims' sense of self-worth, agency, and emotional well-being. By unveiling the intricate mechanisms of narcissistic abuse, the narrative offers solace and validation to survivors while underscoring the universal nature of their experiences. In confronting the painful realities of narcissistic relationships, readers embark on a journey of healing, empowerment, and self-discovery.

LESSONS AND KEY POINTS FROM THIS CHAPTER

1. The author illustrates the complexities of narcissistic abuse through Jordan's narrative, highlighting the profound impact of familial narcissism on personal identity and emotional well-being.

2. Understanding narcissistic traits and behaviors is essential in recognizing the insidious dynamics of narcissistic abuse, which can range from subtle manipulation to overt coercion and control.

3. Gaslighting emerges as a central theme in narcissistic relationships, undermining victims' perceptions of reality and fostering confusion and doubt about their own experiences.

4. The DIMMER patterns—Dismissiveness, Invalidation, Minimization, Manipulation, Exploitativeness, and Rage—illuminate the pervasive mechanisms

through which narcissistic individuals exert dominance and control over their victims.

5. The domination patterns, including Coercive Control, Isolation, Revenge, and Threats, serve as instruments of psychological manipulation and intimidation, perpetuating a cycle of fear and subservience.

6. Disagreeable patterns such as Arguing, Blame-Shifting, and Word Salad further erode victims' sense of agency and self-worth, fueling a cycle of confusion and despair within narcissistic relationships.

7. Love bombing, devaluation, discard, hoovering, and trauma bonds constitute critical phases in the narcissistic relationship cycle, each marked by distinct patterns of manipulation and control.

8. The harm inflicted by narcissistic abuse transcends individual experiences, permeating interpersonal dynamics and leaving lasting scars on victims' psyches. Recognition and validation of survivors' experiences are essential to healing and empowerment.

REFLECTION QUESTIONS

Have you ever felt confused or uncertain about someone's intentions in a relationship or friendship? How did you handle those feelings, and did you notice any patterns of manipulation or control?

Do you often question your memories or perceptions of events, especially when others contradict them? How do you navigate situations where you feel like your reality is being invalidated?

Have you ever experienced moments where you felt like you were walking on eggshells around someone, afraid to express yourself freely? How did this impact your sense of self and emotional well-being?

Can you recall instances where you felt pressured to conform to someone else's expectations or desires, even if it went against your values or beliefs? How did you manage these conflicts, and what did you learn from the experience?

Reflect on your past relationships or interactions where you may have experienced cycles of idealization followed by devaluation or discard. How did these patterns affect your self-esteem and overall perception of love and connection?

MILESTONE GOALS

Readers need to identify signs of narcissistic abuse in their relationships to establish healthy boundaries and protect their emotional well-being.

Readers need to understand the cycle of narcissistic relationships to break free from manipulation, discard, and hoovering tactics employed by narcissistic individuals.

Readers need to recognize trauma bonds and develop strategies to overcome emotional ties that keep them trapped in toxic narcissistic relationships, prioritizing their healing and empowerment.

ACTIONABLE MOVEMENTS

1. **Trust Your Instincts:** If you feel something is off in a relationship, don't dismiss it. Reflect on your feelings and, if needed, seek the advice of trusted friends or family.

2. **Communication Practice:** Work on expressing your boundaries clearly and assertively. Practice saying "no" when necessary and communicate your needs openly.

3. **Supportive Network Building:** Strengthen connections with friends and family who understand your experiences. Share your feelings and seek their support when dealing with challenging relationships.

4. **Educational Journey:** Invest time in learning more about narcissistic behaviour, abuse dynamics, and recovery. Read books, attend workshops, or join support groups to gain valuable insights.

5. **Mindful Self-Care:** Incorporate self-care practices into your routine. Whether meditation, exercise, or creative activities, find what brings you joy and peace, and make it a regular part of your life.

6. **Detoxify Relationships:** Assess your social circles and identify toxic relationships. Consider limiting or cutting ties with individuals who consistently contribute to negative experiences.

7. **Journaling for Reflection:** Keep a journal to document your feelings, experiences and reflections. This can help you recognize patterns, track progress, and clarify your emotions.

8. **Therapeutic Exploration:** If available, consider professional therapy to delve deeper into your experiences, receive guidance, and develop coping strategies tailored to your situation.

9. **Empowerment through Boundaries:** Practice setting and enforcing boundaries in small daily interactions. This can help you build confidence in asserting yourself and protect your emotional well-being.

10. **Focus on Growth:** Channel your energy into personal growth. Set goals, big or small, that align with your values and aspirations. Celebrate your achievement as you reclaim your sense of self.

In the empty pages ahead, you can explore this chapter more deeply and make it your own. Take this opportunity to write your thoughts, ideas, and questions about what you've read so far. Feel free to brainstorm, draw, or note down any questions that pop into your head.

CHAPTER 3:
THE FALLOUT:
THE IMPACT OF
NARCISSISTIC ABUSE

Summary

In the exploration of narcissistic abuse, pain becomes a focal point: how individuals evade it, succumb to it, deal with it, and ultimately transcend it, as reflected in Audre Lorde's poignant statement. The story of Jaya and Ryan encapsulates the intricate dynamics and the profound fallout of narcissistic relationships.

The author uses the story of Jaya and Ryan to illustrate the insidious nature of narcissistic abuse within relationships. Jaya's experience with Ryan unveils a pattern of emotional manipulation, gaslighting, and control that ultimately leaves her feeling exhausted, anxious, and isolated. Despite recognizing the toxicity of the relationship, Jaya struggles to break free from the cycle of false promises and self-blame. Their narrative underscores the devastating toll that narcissistic behavior can exact on an individual's mental and emotional well-being, perpetuating a cycle of psychological anguish and relational turmoil.

Understanding Narcissistic Abuse
Delving deeper into the pervasive impact of narcissistic abuse on individuals, the author elucidates how it infiltrates every facet of their lives. By drawing parallels to trauma, the author emphasizes the profound shifts in self-perception, emotional reactions, and physical health stemming from enduring narcissistic behavior. The erosion of self-worth and autonomy under the weight of manipulation and invalidation underscores the lasting scars inflicted by narcissistic abuse, underscoring the urgent need for validation and healing within survivor communities.

Navigating the Fallout: Healing and Recovery

Shifting the focus from identifying narcissistic individuals to understanding the damaging effects of their behaviour, the author emphasizes the importance of validation and healing for survivors. By acknowledging the trauma bonding and the deep-rooted self-blame, individuals can begin to heal and reclaim their sense of self-worth. Empowering survivors to recognize the toxic dynamics at play fosters a sense of agency and resilience, laying the foundation for transformative healing journeys characterized by self-discovery and renewal.

Phases of Narcissistic Relationships

The author outlines the phases individuals typically experience in narcissistic relationships, from initially asserting themselves to gradually succumbing to self-doubt and hopelessness. By elucidating these phases, the author aims to assuage self-blame and empower survivors to recognize the toxic dynamics. Understanding the cyclical nature of narcissistic abuse illuminates the complexities of emotional entanglement and psychological manipulation, fostering greater awareness and insight into the intricacies of abusive dynamics.

The Fallout of Narcissistic Abuse: Psychological and Emotional Toll

Enumerating the psychological and emotional toll of narcissistic abuse, the author provides insight into the myriad ways individuals experience distress and dysfunction. From rumination and loneliness to depression and suicidal thoughts, the fallout encompasses a spectrum of debilitating effects on one's mental and emotional well-being. The erosion of self-esteem and the fragmentation of identity underpins the profound psychological anguish inflicted by narcissistic abuse, necessitating compassionate support and comprehensive interventions to facilitate healing and recovery.

Coping Mechanisms and Health Implications

The author concludes by addressing the coping mechanisms individuals adopt to manage narcissistic relationships and the detrimental impact on their physical health and well-being. From sleep difficulties to self-care deficits, the toll of narcissistic abuse extends beyond emotional anguish to encompass profound physiological repercussions. Exploring the intersection of psychological distress and somatic symptoms underscores the holistic nature of healing, emphasizing the importance of integrated approaches to address the multifaceted sequelae of narcissistic abuse.

Recognizing the 3 Rs

In understanding the profound impact of narcissistic abuse, survivors often grapple with the pervasive presence of the 3 Rs: regret, rumination, and euphoric recall. These psychological phenomena encapsulate the intricate web of emotions and cognitive processes that characterize the aftermath of narcissistic relationships. By delving deeper into these dimensions, individuals can gain invaluable insights into their healing journey and reclaim agency over their lives.

Regret

Regret, a poignant facet of post-narcissistic trauma, embodies the myriad of what-ifs and could-have-been that haunt survivors long after the relationship has ended. It serves as a sobering reminder of the missed opportunities, misplaced trust, and unfulfilled aspirations that defined their journey with the narcissistic individual. From lamenting the loss of self to grappling with the erosion of personal boundaries, regret underscores the profound disillusionment and betrayal permeating survivors' narratives.

The author elucidates how regret often becomes entwined with self-blame, fostering a toxic cycle of introspection and recrimination. Whether questioning one's judgment or mourning the dissolution of cherished dreams, survivors navigate a labyrinth of conflicting emotions as they confront the wreckage left in the wake of narcissistic abuse. Despite the inherent challenges, acknowledging and processing feelings of regret can catalyze transformative growth and pave the path toward healing and self-discovery.

Rumination

Rumination, akin to an ongoing mental echo, amplifies the complexities of narcissistic trauma by ensnaring survivors in a relentless cycle of self-reflection and doubt. It manifests as a relentless pursuit of meaning and validation within a relationship defined by manipulation and gaslighting. From replaying past conversations to dissecting perceived missteps, rumination becomes a pervasive force that eclipses moments of joy and connection in survivors' lives.

The author underscores how rumination serves as both a coping mechanism and a barrier to healing, perpetuating feelings of isolation and disconnection from the present moment. By shedding light on the insidious nature of rumination, survivors can cultivate greater self-awareness and resilience in navigating the tumultuous terrain of recovery. Through mindfulness practices and therapeutic interventions, individuals can gradually disentangle themselves from the grip of rumination, forging a path toward emotional liberation and renewal.

Euphoric Recall

Euphoric recall, a bittersweet reverie of past happiness, casts a luminous glow amidst the shadowy contours of narcissistic abuse. It represents a paradoxical fusion of longing and disillusionment as survivors navigate the juxtaposition of cherished memories and harsh realities. Despite the pervasive invalidation and manipulation, euphoric recall offers a fleeting reprieve from the tumultuous landscape of post traumatic recovery.

The author elucidates how euphoric recall serves as a double-edged sword, blurring the boundaries between truth and illusion within the context of narcissistic relationships. While evoking feelings of nostalgia and warmth, it also perpetuate a cycle of longing and despair, trapping survivors in a perpetual quest for closure and validation. By confronting the illusions of euphoric recall with courage and self-awareness, individuals can reclaim agency over their narratives and embark on a journey of authentic self-discovery and empowerment.

Self-Blame

At the heart of narcissistic trauma lies the insidious specter of self-blame, a pervasive force that corrodes self-esteem and erodes personal agency. Rooted in the dynamics of gaslighting and manipulation, self-blame emerges as a reflexive response to the complexities of narcissistic relationships. It represents a profound internalization of guilt and shame as survivors grapple with the burden of holding themselves accountable for the actions of others.

The author unpacks the intricate interplay of emotions and cognitive processes that perpetuate self-blame, tracing its origins to childhood experiences of betrayal and invalidation. From internalizing parental expectations to shouldering the weight of familial dysfunction, individuals navigate a treacherous terrain of self-criticism and doubt within narcissistic relationships. By challenging distorted narratives and reclaiming personal autonomy, survivors can transcend the shackles of self-blame and embrace a journey of self-compassion and resilience.

Shame

Shame permeates the aftermath of narcissistic abuse, leaving individuals feeling damaged, broken, and irredeemable. The author illustrates shame as a public manifestation of self-blame, reinforcing the belief that one is inherently flawed and unworthy. Drawing from experiences within narcissistic families, where "not good enough" becomes a prevailing mantra, the author elucidates how shame becomes ingrained from an early age. The narrative delves into the isolating effects of shame, perpetuating a cycle of secrecy, false narratives, and internalized self-blame. In essence, individuals become repositories for the shame projected onto them by narcissistic figures, perpetuating a cycle of emotional turmoil and self-negation.

Confusion

The author delves into the pervasive confusion experienced by individuals navigating narcissistic relationships, characterized by a profound sense of disorientation and self-doubt. Drawing from firsthand accounts, the author explores the bewildering dichotomy of narcissistic behavior, from expressions of love to acts of invalidation and betrayal. The narrative underscores the insidious nature of gaslighting and manipulation, which erode one's sense of reality and self-trust. Triangulation emerges as a potent manipulation tool, fostering mistrust and discord within relationships. The author emphasizes the destabilizing impact of confusion, which undermines one's sense of identity and agency, perpetuating a cycle of psychological entrapment.

Despair

Despair looms large in the wake of narcissistic relationships, encompassing a spectrum of emotions from sadness and helplessness to hopelessness and suicidal thoughts. The author elucidates the bleak realization that narcissistic individuals lack genuine empathy and prioritize their needs above all else. The narrative underscores the pervasive powerlessness and grief stemming from recognizing that the relationship cannot change. Despair extends beyond the individual, impacting familial, professional, and social spheres and exacerbating feelings of isolation and emotional distress. The author underscores the importance of recognizing depressive patterns and seeking mental health support amidst the tumult of narcissistic abuse.

In concluding the discourse on narcissistic abuse, the author underscores the imperative of healing, growth, and resilience. Despite the pervasive fallout of narcissistic relationships, the author affirms that recovery is possible, offering hope and encouragement to survivors. The narrative shifts focus from survival to thriving and flourishing, empowering individuals to reclaim agency, self-understanding, and clarity. Through introspection, support, and self-compassion, survivors can transcend the trauma of narcissistic abuse, emerging stronger, wiser, and infused with newfound purpose. As the discourse evolves from acknowledgment to action, the journey toward healing becomes a beacon of hope, illuminating pathways to authentic self-expression and enduring resilience.

LESSONS AND KEY POINTS FROM THIS CHAPTER

1. The author uses Jaya and Ryan's story to illustrate the devastating toll of narcissistic abuse, highlighting emotional manipulation, gaslighting, and isolation

2. Understanding the pervasive impact of narcissistic abuse involves recognizing its parallels to trauma and its erosion of self-worth and autonomy.

3. Healing from narcissistic abuse requires validating survivors' experiences empowering them to reclaim agency, and fostering transformative growth.

4. The phases of narcissistic relationships involve initial assertion, gradual self-doubt, and eventual despair, underscoring the cyclical nature of abuse.

5. The psychological and emotional fallout from narcissistic abuse includes rumination, loneliness, depression, and suicidal thoughts, necessitating comprehensive support and intervention.

6. Coping mechanisms adopted in narcissistic relationships often lead to detrimental health implications, such as sleep difficulties and self-care deficits.

7. Survivors grapple with regret, rumination, and euphoric recall, navigating a complex web of emotions and cognitive processes in the aftermath of abuse.

8. Shame perpetuates feelings of unworthiness and self-blame, isolating individuals within a cycle of emotional turmoil and secrecy.

9. Confusion arises from gaslighting and manipulation in narcissistic relationships, eroding reality and self-trust through triangulation and invalidation.

10. Despair pervades the aftermath of narcissistic relationships, fueling feelings of powerlessness, grief, and emotional isolation, underscoring the importance of seeking mental health support and validation.

REFLECTION QUESTIONS

Reflecting on your past relationships, have you noticed any patterns of manipulation or emotional abuse that resemble narcissistic behavior?

How do you cope with regret and self-blame after a challenging relationship or experience?

Have you ever doubted your reality or perceptions due to someone else's gaslighting or invalidation?

What strategies do you employ to maintain your sense of self-worth and autonomy in relationships, especially when faced with manipulation or control tactics?

How do you prioritize your mental and emotional well-being in the face of adversity, and what steps can you take to cultivate resilience and healing in your journey forward?

MILESTONE GOALS

- Readers need to recognize the signs of narcissistic abuse and understand its impact on mental and emotional well-being to establish healthier boundaries and relationships.

- Readers need to develop coping mechanisms to navigate feelings of regret, self-blame, and confusion stemming from narcissistic relationships, fostering resilience and emotional healing.

- Readers need to prioritize self-care and seek support from mental health professionals to address the psychological fallout of narcissistic abuse, promoting long-term healing and recovery.

ACTIONABLE MOVEMENTS

1. **Self-Education:** Dedicate weekly time to reading books and articles about narcissistic behavior and its impact. Set aside specific times for learning, such as during your lunch break or before bed.

2. **Self-Reflection:** Schedule regular sessions of self-reflection where you journal about your past experiences in relationships. Take note of any patterns or red flags you recognize and consider how they affect your well-being.

3. **Establish Boundaries:** Identify areas where you need to set healthier boundaries with others. Practice saying "no" when you feel uncomfortable or overwhelmed and communicate your boundaries assertively but respectfully.

4. **Seek Support:** Reach out to a therapist or counselor specializing in trauma and abuse. Schedule regular sessions to discuss your experiences and work through any lingering emotions or challenges.

5. **Develop Coping Strategies:** Experiment with different coping strategies to manage difficult emotions, deep breathing exercises, or engaging in creative hobbies. Find what works best for you and incorporate it into your daily routine.

6. **Practice Self-Care:** Prioritise self-care by scheduling regular activities that bring joy and relaxation. This could include anything from taking long walks in nature to treating yourself to a spa day or indulging in your favorite hobbies.

7. **Set Boundaries with Narcissistic Individuals:** Evaluate your relationships and consider whether any of them are toxic or unhealthy. If necessary, distance yourself from individuals who exhibit narcissistic behavior and surround yourself with supportive and empathetic people instead.

8. **Seek Professional Help:** If you're struggling to cope independently, don't hesitate to seek professional help. Reach out to a therapist, counselor, or support group in your area for the support and guidance you need.

9. **Educate Others:** Share what you've learned about narcissistic abuse with friends and loved ones. Help raise awareness about the signs and effects of narcissistic behavior so that others can recognize it and seek help if needed.

10. **Focus on Growth and Healing:** Remember that healing from narcissistic abuse takes time and patience. Be gentle with yourself as you navigate this journey and celebrate each milestone. Stay focused on your growth and well-being, and know that you deserve love, respect, and happiness.

In the empty pages ahead, you can explore this chapter more deeply and make it your own. Take this opportunity to write your thoughts, ideas, and questions about what you've read so far. Feel free to brainstorm, draw, or note down any questions that pop into your head.

PART II: RECOGNITION, RECOVERY, HEALING, AND GROWTH

CHAPTER 4: UNDERSTAND YOUR BACKSTORY

Summary

In this chapter, the author observes that individuals often find themselves entangled in intricate webs of emotions and behaviors. Sarah's journey, marked by liberation from past toxicity and the promise of new beginnings upon her relocation to Los Angeles, is a poignant example. However, her encounter with Josh, initially just a friend, unraveled unforeseen layers of vulnerability and Resilience, shedding light on the complexities of human connection.

Sarah's relocation to Los Angeles marked a pivotal moment, offering liberation from past toxicity and the promise of new beginnings. However, her encounter with Josh initially just a friend, unraveled unforeseen layers of vulnerability and Resilience. As Sarah embarked on her journey of self-discovery, navigating the unfamiliar terrain of Los Angeles, she found solace and struggle in her burgeoning relationship with Josh. The author reflects on Sarah's narrative, recognizing the intricate dynamics of vulnerability and Resilience at play, and delves into the complexities of healing from narcissistic entanglements.

Sarah's narrative prompts a critical inquiry into the allure of narcissistic individual and the challenges of disentanglement. As individuals navigate the intricate landscape of relationships, they often encounter unexpected vulnerabilities that shape their interactions and perceptions. The author delves into the complexities of healing emphasizing the importance of introspection and self-awareness in unraveling the intricacies of narcissistic entanglements. Sarah's journey serves as a poignant reminder of the multifaceted nature of vulnerability and Resilience in navigating complex interpersonal dynamics.

Understanding Vulnerabilities

The author navigates through the labyrinth of vulnerabilities, exploring the magnetic allure of narcissistic traits and the intricacies of empathic resonance. Sarah's empathy and inclination towards rescuing reflect common pathways to entrapment in narcissistic relationships. By examining the interplay between individual vulnerabilities and external influences, the author sheds light on the nuanced dynamics that underpin narcissistic entanglements. Through introspection and understanding, individuals can unravel the intricacies of their vulnerabilities, forging a path toward healing and self-discovery.

The Empathy Trap

Empathy emerges as both a beacon of compassion and a potential pitfall, blurring the lines between support and exploitation. Sarah's unwavering empathy for Josh underscores the struggle to reconcile kindness with self-preservation. As individuals navigate the complexities of empathy and compassion, they must confront the inherent risks of emotional entanglement in narcissistic relationships. Individuals can safeguard against the empathy trap by cultivating awareness and setting boundaries while fostering genuine connections rooted in mutual respect and understanding.

The Rescuer's Dilemma

Rescuers like Sarah epitomize the paradox of altruism, caught between the compulsion to fix and the realization of futility. The author dissects the rescue narrative, highlighting its perilous descent into enabling and codependency. Sarah's journey serves as a poignant reminder of the delicate balance between compassion and self-preservation in navigating narcissistic relationships. By recognizing the inherent risks of the rescuer's dilemma, individuals can cultivate healthy boundaries and prioritize their well-being while extending support to others.

Optimism and Resilience

Optimism emerges as a double-edged sword, offering Resilience in adversity yet concealing the harsh realities of unchangeable behavior. Sarah's unwavering optimism mirrors the delicate balance between hope and disillusionment. As individuals confront the complexities of optimism and Resilience, they must grapple with the inherent challenges of navigating narcissistic relationships. By embracing vulnerability and fostering Resilience, individuals can navigate the tumultuous terrain of interpersonal dynamics with grace and fortitude, forging a path toward healing and self-discovery.

Being Forever Forgiving

The author uses Sarah's story to illustrate the intricate dynamics of forgiveness, especially within narcissistic relationships. In many contexts, forgiveness is seen as a virtue—a sign of maturity and compassion. However, when extended to narcissistic individuals, forgiveness can become a vulnerability rather than a strength. Sarah's experience with Josh highlights how forgiveness can inadvertently reinforce toxic behaviors instead of prompting positive change. Despite not actively forgiving Josh for his transgressions, Sarah's reluctance to address his behavior and her willingness to make allowances contributed to a cycle of betrayal and manipulation. This cycle, fueled by the absence of meaningful consequences and the expectation of forgiveness, perpetuated Sarah's entanglement in a harmful relationship.

Narcissistic, Antagonistic, or Invalidating Parents

The author delves into the lasting impact of growing up in a narcissistic family system, drawing attention to the pervasive sense of invalidation and self-blame experienced by individuals raised in such environments. Through Sarah's narrative, the author underscores how narcissistic family dynamics normalize toxic behaviors, instilling in children a skewed perception of love and self-worth. Children in narcissistic families often find themselves fulfilling specific roles dictated by the needs of the narcissistic parent, further perpetuating a cycle of dysfunction and emotional manipulation. Sarah's empathy towards Josh, rooted in her own experiences of invalidation, exemplifies how early familial dynamics shape interpersonal relationships in adulthood, rendering individuals more susceptible to narcissistic entanglements.

Happy Families

The author explores the paradoxical vulnerability of individuals raised in ostensibly happy families, where love and support abound. Through the lens of Sarah's story, the author highlights how the absence of conflict and adversity in childhood can leave individuals ill-equipped to recognize and address toxic behaviors in adult relationships. Raised in an environment characterized by empathy and compassion individuals from happy families may struggle to reconcile the presence of narcissistic traits in their partners, clinging to the belief that love conquers all. Sarah's experience underscores the pervasive influence of familial upbringing on adult relationships challenging the notion that happy families are immune to narcissistic dynamics.

Difficult Transitions

Transitions, whether marked by trauma or aspiration, emerge as fertile ground for vulnerability in the realm of narcissistic relationships. The author reflects on Sarah's tumultuous relocation journey and personal upheaval, highlighting how transition periods can amplify feelings of vulnerability and disorientation. Amidst the chaos of change, individuals may find solace in newfound connections, unwittingly exposing themselves to the manipulative tactics of narcissistic individuals. Sarah's encounter with Josh during a period of transition illustrates how vulnerability can pave the way for entanglement in toxic relationships, underscoring the importance of self awareness and caution during times of change.

Rushed Relationships

The author examines the perils of rushed relationships, where external pressures and personal timelines overshadow discernment and self-preservation. Drawing from real-life anecdotes, the author emphasizes how the urgency to fulfill societal expectations or personal goals can blind individuals to red flags and warning signs in potential partners. Sarah's haste in transitioning from friendship to romance with Josh reflects the impulsive nature of rushed relationships, characterized by love bombing and accelerated milestones. Individuals risk entrenching themselves in toxic dynamics that erode their well-being and autonomy by prioritizing immediate gratification over long-term compatibility.

History of Trauma, Betrayal, or Significant Loss

The author delves into the profound impact of trauma and betrayal on individuals' susceptibility to narcissistic relationships, highlighting the enduring psychological scars left by experiences of loss and betrayal. Through Sarah's narrative, the author illuminates how unresolved trauma and betrayal trauma can distort perceptions of self-worth and trust, rendering individuals more vulnerable to exploitation and manipulation. Sarah's own struggles with self-doubt and emotional pain mirror the profound toll of past trauma on interpersonal relationships, underscoring the importance of trauma-informed therapy and self-compassion in the journey toward healing and Resilience.

The Narcissistic Family System

In dissecting the dynamics of narcissistic family systems, the author offers a poignant exploration of familial roles and their lasting impact on individual identity and relationships. Through the lens of the Smith family's dysfunction, the author illustrates how narcissistic parents exploit familial dynamics to maintain control and perpetuate cycles of abuse and manipulation. Each family member's role, from the scapegoat to the golden child, reflects the insidious ways in which narcissistic parents shape their children's identities and perpetuate dysfunction. Sarah's experiences resonate with the pervasive influence of familial roles on adult relationships, underscoring the importance of self-awareness and boundary-setting in breaking free from familial patterns of dysfunction.

The Golden Child

The author highlights the intricate dynamics surrounding the role of the golden child within narcissistic family structures. Through the lens of Sheryl's experience, who embodied the part of the golden child in the Smith family, the author elucidates how the golden child serves as a vital source of validation and admiration for the narcissistic parent. Sheryl's narrative underscores the conditional nature of the golden child's pedestal, fraught with the constant pressure to maintain performance and validation. The author delves into the psychological complexities faced by empathic golden children, navigating the delicate balance between privilege and guilt. Furthermore, the author emphasizes the importance of recognizing and addressing the impact of the golden child's role on familial dynamics and individual well-being.

The Scapegoat

The author delves into the profound ramifications of the scapegoat role within narcissistic family dynamics, drawing upon Diane's experiences in the Smith family as a poignant example. Through Diane's narrative, the author explores the harrowing realities faced by scapegoated children, including psychological abuse, disproportionate blame, and emotional neglect. The scapegoat's narrative serves as a stark reminder of the enduring trauma and psychological scars inflicted by narcissistic parenting. By shedding light on the complexities of scapegoating, the author advocates for trauma-informed therapy and self-advocacy as essential tools for healing and recovery.

The Helper

Through Thomas's narrative of the Smith family, the author unpacks the nuanced role of the helper within narcissistic family dynamics. Thomas's experiences shed light on the burdensome responsibilities shouldered by helper children, from caretaking to emotional appeasement. The author underscores the distinction between genuine support and coercive caregiving, emphasizing the detrimental impact of prolonged immersion in the helper role. By empowering individuals to set boundaries and reclaim agency, the author advocates for self-liberation from the confines of the helper archetype.

The Fixer/Peacekeeper

The author navigates through the intricate role of the fixer/peacekeeper within narcissistic family systems, drawing upon Andrew's experiences in the Smith family as a poignant illustration. Andrew's narrative illuminates the perpetual tension between conflict avoidance and emotional labor inherent in the fixer role. The author underscores the toll of chronic vigilance and emotional exhaustion experienced by fixers, urging individuals to prioritize self-care and boundary-setting. By fostering self-awareness and Resilience, individuals can navigate the complexities of familial dynamics with grace and autonomy.

The Invisible Child

Martine's narrative within the Smith family serves as a compelling backdrop for exploring the plight of the invisible child within narcissistic family structures. The author delves into the profound sense of neglect and invisibility experienced by invisible children, emphasizing the detrimental impact on self-esteem and identity formation. The author advocates self-advocacy and boundary-setting through Martine's story as essential mechanisms for reclaiming agency and autonomy. By embracing self-validation and cultivating healthy relationships, invisible children can transcend the confines of familial neglect and embark on a journey of self-discovery.

The Truth Seer/Teller

Through Thomas's journey within the Smith family, the author examines the transformative power of truth-telling within narcissistic family dynamics. Thomas narrative illuminates the inherent conflict between truth-telling and familial loyalty, underscoring the profound sense of isolation and grief experienced by truth-seers. By fostering self-compassion and cultivating a supportive network, truth seers can navigate the complexities of familial estrangement with Resilience and grace. The author advocates for trauma-informed therapy and community support as essential tools for healing and self-empowerment.

Understanding Backstories

The author emphasizes the importance of understanding one's backstory and vulnerabilities while navigating narcissistic relationships. It's essential to recognize that some of the most admirable traits in oneself might paradoxically make one susceptible to toxic relationships. The author uses the story of Sarah and her journey to illustrate this point. Sarah's empathetic nature and her inclination to fix things served as both her strength and vulnerability, drawing her into a narcissistic relationship with Josh.

Unveiling Enabling Systems

The author sheds light on the broader societal and familial systems that enable narcissistic behaviors. In narcissistic family systems, the dynamic often revolves around silence and denial, where calling out a narcissistic member is met with resistance or gaslighting. Similarly, workplaces may foster narcissism by rewarding high performers at the expense of toxic behavior. By examining these enabling systems, the author highlights the challenges survivors face in healing within contexts that perpetuate narcissistic patterns.

Despite being aware of one's backstory and vulnerabilities, healing within broken systems presents a daunting challenge. The author underscores the Resilience required to navigate narcissistic relationships while advocating for systemic change. Survivors like Sarah must learn to heal amidst societal structures that perpetuate narcissistic patterns, recognizing that the journey toward healing is an ongoing process.

Practicing Contrary Actions and Setting Boundaries

Survivors can challenge ingrained patterns by practicing contrary actions and setting boundaries. Individuals can reclaim agency in their relationships by consciously resisting the urge to fix or rescue. Setting clear boundaries is a protective mechanism, guiding survivors towards healthier dynamics while fostering self-awareness and autonomy.

Accessing safe spaces and seeking trauma-informed therapy are vital steps in the healing journey. By surrounding themselves with supportive networks, survivors can cultivate Resilience and challenge limiting beliefs ingrained by narcissistic relationships. Education about narcissism empowers survivors to recognize unhealthy behaviors and advocate for their well-being within their social circles.

Embracing Growth and Radical Acceptance

Healing from narcissistic abuse entails embracing growth and radical acceptance of one's authentic self. Survivors are encouraged to confront core wounds and redefine their identities outside toxic relationships. By acknowledging their strengths and vulnerabilities, survivors embark on self-discovery and empowerment, laying the foundation for meaningful growth and individuation.

In conclusion, understanding one's backstory, vulnerabilities, and the dynamics of narcissistic relationships is pivotal in the journey toward healing. Survivors must navigate enabling systems, and practice discernment to reclaim agency and autonomy. By embracing growth and radical acceptance, survivors embark on a transformative journey towards self-discovery and empowerment, forging a path towards healing from narcissistic abuse.

LESSONS AND KEY POINTS FROM THIS CHAPTER

1. **The author delves into Understanding Vulnerabilities:** Sarah's narrative unveils the complexities of vulnerability and Resilience, urging introspection and self-awareness to navigate narcissistic entanglements effectively.

2. **The book warns of the Empathy Trap:** Empathy, while noble, can become a pitfall, blurring boundaries and perpetuating toxic relationships, emphasizing the need for discernment and self-preservation.

3. **The author tackles The Rescuer's Dilemma:** Rescuers like Sarah confront the paradox of altruism, balancing compassion with self-care amidst the cycle of enabling and codependency.

4. **Optimism and Resilience are explored:** Optimism offers Resilience but can obscure toxic behaviour, highlighting the importance of cautious optimism and self-preservation in navigating narcissistic dynamics.

5. **Being Forever Forgiving is cautioned:** Forgiveness, though virtuous, can perpetuate toxicity when extended to narcissistic individuals, underscoring the necessity of setting boundaries and prioritizing self-respect.

6. **The impact of Narcissistic, Antagonistic, or Invalidating Parents is discussed** Familial dynamics shape vulnerability, illustrating the lasting impact of narcissistic family systems on adult relationships.

7. **Happy Families may overlook toxic behaviours:** Ostensibly happy families may overlook toxic behaviours, challenging perceptions of familial love and support in navigating narcissistic relationships.

8. **Difficult Transitions amplify vulnerability:** Transition periods amplify vulnerability, emphasizing the importance of caution and self-awareness in forming new connections amidst change.

9. **Rushed Relationships fuel toxicity:** External pressures fuel rushed relationships, obscuring red flags and eroding autonomy, necessitating discernment and patience in forming meaningful connections.

10. **History of Trauma, Betrayal, or Significant Loss magnifies susceptibility:** Past trauma magnifies susceptibility to narcissistic relationships, highlighting the role of trauma-informed therapy and self-compassion in healing.

REFLECTION QUESTIONS

Have you ever found yourself repeatedly drawn to people who seem charming but end up causing you emotional harm? Reflect on why you might be attracted to such individuals and how to break this pattern.

Do you often feel the need to rescue or fix others, even at the expense of your well-being? Consider the motivations behind your actions and whether they stem from a genuine desire to help or a deeper need for validation.

How do you navigate conflicts and disagreements in your relationships? Reflect on whether you prioritize harmony over addressing underlying issues and how this approach may impact the dynamics of your relationships.

What role does forgiveness play in your life, especially in the context of toxic or abusive relationships? Consider whether your willingness to forgive has empowered you to move forward or inadvertently enabled harmful behaviour to persist.

How do you practice self-care and set boundaries in your relationships? Reflect on whether you prioritize your needs and well-being, and identify areas where you can strengthen your borders to cultivate healthier dynamics.

MILESTONE GOALS

- Readers need to gain a deeper understanding of their vulnerabilities and past experiences that may make them susceptible to narcissistic relationships. By reflecting on their personal histories and emotional triggers, readers can identify patterns and take proactive steps to protect themselves from toxic dynamics in the future.

- Another goal is for readers to cultivate mindfulness and discernment in their interactions. By slowing down and paying attention to red flags or manipulative behaviors, readers can make more informed decisions about whom to trust and how to navigate complex relationships.

- Readers must also prioritize self-care and seek support from trusted individuals or professionals. By acknowledging the impact of narcissistic abuse on their well-being, readers can take steps to prioritize their mental and emotional health, set boundaries, and foster Resilience in the face of adversity.

ACTIONABLE MOVEMENTS

1. **Create a Self-Reflection Routine:** Set aside 10-15 minutes each evening to reflect on your interactions, emotions, and experiences throughout the day. Consider keeping a journal where you can jot down your thoughts, insights, and observations.

2. **Practice Mindful Breathing:** Dedicate a few minutes each morning to practice mindful breathing exercises. Find a quiet space, sit comfortably, and focus on your breath. Inhale deeply through your nose, hold for a moment, and exhale slowly through your mouth. Repeat this process several times, allowing yourself to become fully present in the moment.

3. **Establish Clear Boundaries:** Identify areas where your boundaries are being crossed or where you must set firmer limits. Communicate your boundaries assertively and respectfully to those involved. Practice saying "no" when necessary and prioritize your well-being.

4. **Reach Out for Support:** Take the initiative to contact a trusted friend, family member, or therapist to discuss your experiences and emotions. Schedule regular check-ins or therapy sessions to process your feelings, gain perspective, and receive validation and support.

5. **Educate Yourself:** Dedicate time each week to educate yourself about narcissism, healthy relationship dynamics, and trauma recovery. Utilize resources such as books, online articles, podcasts, and support groups to deepen your understanding and gain practical insights into navigating challenging situations.

6. **Engage in Self-Care Activities:** Identify self-care practices that resonate with you and incorporate them into your daily routine. This could include taking a warm bath, walking in nature, or engaging in creative hobbies.

7. **Set Achievable Goals:** Break down your healing journey into smaller, manageable goals that you can work towards gradually. Celebrate your progress along the way and adjust your goals as needed based on your evolving needs and priorities.

8. **Practice Assertive Communication:** Work on expressing your thoughts, feelings, and boundaries clearly and assertively. Practice using "I" statements to communicate your needs and preferences while respecting the perspectives of others.

9. **Create a Support Network:** Cultivate relationships with individuals who uplift and support you on your journey towards healing. Surround yourself with people who validate your experiences, encourage you, and offer constructive feedback when needed.

10. **Celebrate Your Growth:** Take time to acknowledge and celebrate your progress in your healing journey. Celebrate milestones, no matter how small, and recognize the resilience and strength you've demonstrated.

In the empty pages ahead, you can explore this chapter more deeply and make it your own. Take this opportunity to write your thoughts, ideas, and questions about what you've read so far. Feel free to brainstorm, draw, or note down any questions that pop into your head.

CHAPTER 5: EMBRACE RADICAL ACCEPTANCE

Summary

In the intricate landscape of human relationships, the dynamics of narcissism often present profound challenges. Navigating these relationships requires a nuanced understanding of self and others, particularly when confronted with the unyielding nature of narcissistic behavior. Through stories and insights, the concept of radical acceptance emerges as a beacon of hope and transformation, offering a pathway toward healing and growth amidst the complexities of narcissistic relationships.

The story of the scorpion and the swan serves as a poignant allegory for the inherent nature of certain individuals. Just as the scorpion's instinctual drive to sting ultimately prevails over its promises, narcissistic individuals exhibit a similar pattern of behavior despite outward charm and persuasion. The author highlights the deceptive allure of narcissistic personalities and underscores the importance of recognizing the inevitability of their actions to navigate relationships with clarity and resilience.

The Power of Radical Acceptance

Through the lived experiences of individuals like Luisa and Costa, the transformative potential of radical acceptance comes into focus. Luisa's decades-long journey in narcissistic relationship and Costa's internal struggle with self-worth epitomize the profound impact of embracing radical acceptance. Their stories illuminate the pivotal moment of realization, where the veil of denial is lifted, and acceptance becomes the catalyst for personal liberation and empowerment.

Radical Acceptance Is the Gateway to Healing

In recounting the journey of a client grappling with the complexities of narcissistic behavior, the author delves into the transformative nature of radical acceptance. By acknowledging the limitations of control and embracing acceptance, individuals can transcend the cycle of self-blame and reclaim agency over their emotional well-being. Through radical acceptance, healing becomes not merely a destination but a profound journey of self-discovery and resilience.

The Barriers to Radical Acceptance

The journey towards radical acceptance is fraught with internal and external barriers, chief among them being the lingering hope for change and the fear of confronting uncomfortable truths. The author explores the intricacies of guilt, denial, and societal expectations that often impede the process of acceptance. Individuals can embark on a transformative journey towards healing and self-empowerment by unraveling these barriers and fostering a sense of self-compassion.

Overcoming Barriers and Embracing Radical Acceptance

In confronting the challenges of radical acceptance, individuals are urged to redefine their perceptions of worth and agency. By separating narcissistic behavior from intrinsic self-worth, individuals can cultivate a sense of resilience and empowerment in the face of adversity. Through reframing narratives and embracing vulnerability, the journey toward radical acceptance becomes a testament to the strength of the human spirit and the transformative power of self-discovery.

In essence, radical acceptance emerges as a beacon of hope and resilience amidst the complexities of narcissistic relationships. Through introspection, compassion, and self-empowerment, individuals can embark on a journey of healing and transformation, reclaiming agency over their lives and embracing the fullness of their authentic selves.

Radical Acceptance If You Stay

In this section, the author illustrates the story of Emma, who struggled with toxic relationships, including her marriage and her relationship with her mother. Despite Emma's efforts to communicate and seek understanding, she faced manipulation, rage, and disappointment from her husband and mother. Emma's journey reflects the challenges of staying in narcissistic relationships, where hope for change often leads to grief and acceptance of unchangeable circumstances.

The author emphasizes the importance of radical acceptance in acknowledging the realities of narcissistic behavior. For individuals like Emma, who choose to stay in such relationships due to financial constraints or familial ties, radical acceptance becomes a tool for setting boundaries, managing expectations, and prioritizing self-care. By accepting the limitations of these relationships, individuals can navigate through conflicts with resilience and find freedom in embracing their authentic selves.

Radical Acceptance If You Leave

Transitioning to leaving narcissistic relationships, the author highlights the complexities of post-separation dynamics, including hoovering, smear campaigns and manipulation. Through the story of individuals navigating divorce or separation from narcissistic partners, the author underscores the importance of radical acceptance in preparing for the challenges that unfold after leaving the relationship.

Radical acceptance becomes a crucial tool in recognizing the patterns of narcissistic behavior that persist post-separation. Despite the initial doubts and struggles faced after leaving, radical acceptance fortifies individuals' resolve and validates their experiences. By accepting the inevitability of post-separation abuse and maintaining realistic expectations, individuals can navigate the healing process with clarity and self-compassion.

Don't Burn Your Umbrellas: What Are Realistic Expectations for a Narcissistic Relationship?

In this section, the author explores the concept of realistic expectations as the cornerstone of radical acceptance in both staying and leaving narcissistic relationships. By understanding the consistent patterns of narcissistic behavior, individuals can anticipate and prepare for the challenges they will face, whether they choose to stay or leave.

The author emphasizes the need to maintain boundaries, manage information, and prioritize self-care amidst the storms of narcissistic abuse. Realistic expectations serve as a compass for navigating through the complexities of narcissistic relationships and the healing journey after that. By acknowledging the reality of healing as a nonlinear process, individuals can cultivate resilience and find solace in their journey toward self-discovery and emotional well-being.

Tools for Fostering Radical Acceptance

In this section, the author introduces various techniques aimed at promoting radical acceptance in dealing with narcissistic relationships. These tools serve as practical strategies for individuals to confront toxic patterns, validate their experiences, and cultivate a deeper understanding of acceptance amidst challenging circumstances. By implementing these tools, individuals can navigate and cope with the complexities of relationships affected by narcissistic behavior.

Entering the Tiger's Cage: A Pathway for Radical Acceptance

The author introduces the concept of entering the tiger's cage as a metaphor for confronting toxic patterns in relationships with narcissistic individuals. By directly communicating needs and observing responses, individuals can discern whether the relationship involves narcissistic abuse or healthy interaction. This process facilitates radical acceptance by acknowledging and validating one's experiences. Through intentional engagement with the relationship dynamics, individuals gain clarity and insight into their interactions, enabling them to make informed decisions about their well-being.

Don't Hit Send

The author advises against sending lengthy explanations or grievances to narcissistic individuals. Instead, individuals are encouraged to write down their thoughts and feelings as a form of catharsis without intending to send the message. Sharing these writings in a safe space allows individuals to receive empathy and validation for their experiences, fostering radical acceptance through acknowledgment and release. By refraining from engaging in futile attempts to communicate with narcissistic individuals, individuals can prioritize their emotional well-being and focus on constructive self-expression.

The Lists

The author emphasizes the importance of documenting harmful relationship patterns and experiences through lists. The "Ick List" records negative behaviors and events, validating individuals' experiences and countering euphoric recall. Additionally, the "Biscuits in Bed" and "It's My Turn" lists encourage individuals to reclaim autonomy and pursue personal aspirations, fostering radical acceptance through self-care and empowerment. Through the process of list-making, individuals gain clarity and insight into the impact of narcissistic behavior on their lives, enabling them to cultivate resilience and pursue meaningful growth.

Lean into the Rumination

The author acknowledges rumination as a significant challenge in recovering from narcissistic abuse. Rather than attempting to suppress rumination, individuals are encouraged to embrace it by discussing their thoughts and feelings with supportive individuals, such as therapists, friends, or support groups. By externalizing and expressing their rumination, individuals can gradually release their hold on their minds and facilitate the process of healing.

The Toxic Cleanup

The author highlights the presence of multiple toxic individuals in one's life beyond just the primary narcissistic figures. By setting boundaries, ending unhealthy relationships, and embracing radical acceptance, individuals can extend their self-care practices to encompass all areas of their social circle. Cleaning out toxic relationships and minimizing engagement with negative influences are essential steps in fostering emotional well-being and radical acceptance.

Stacking Multiple Truths

Radical acceptance involves acknowledging the complexity of one's emotions and experiences, even when they seem contradictory. By embracing the coexistence of multiple truths, individuals can navigate the cognitive dissonance inherent in narcissistic relationships and gain a holistic understanding of their circumstances.

Stacking truths enables individuals to validate their experiences and emotion without resorting to self-denial or rationalization.

Radically Accepting Yourself
The author emphasizes the importance of extending radical acceptance to oneself. Individuals can cultivate self-compassion and self-acceptance by recognizing and embracing their strengths, vulnerabilities, and preferences. Radical self-acceptance involves acknowledging one's inherent worthiness and refraining from self-judgment or comparison to others. Through this process, individuals can foster a more profound sense of self-awareness and resilience in the face of narcissistic dynamics.

Building radical acceptance is a transformative journey that requires individuals to confront the harsh realities of narcissistic relationships and embrace their inherent worthiness. By leaning into rumination, engaging in toxic cleanup, stacking multiple truths, and radically accepting themselves, individuals can reclaim agency over their lives and begin the process of healing. Radical acceptance serves as a powerful tool for separating from the harmful dynamics of narcissistic relationships and upholding one's well-being. While the journey may be fraught with grief and challenges, radical acceptance paves the way for profound healing and self-discovery. In the next chapter, individuals will explore strategies for processing the sense of loss and grief that often accompanies the end of narcissistic relationships.

LESSONS AND KEY POINTS FROM THIS CHAPTER

1. The author emphasizes embracing radical acceptance as pivotal in navigating narcissistic relationships and reclaiming emotional well-being and personal growth.

2. The book underscores the importance of recognizing the inevitability of narcissistic behavior to navigate relationships with clarity and resilience, transcending cycles of self-blame and denial.

3. The author identifies internal barriers like hope for change and fear of uncomfortable truths, urging introspection and self-compassion to overcome them on the journey to radical acceptance.

4. The book highlights setting realistic expectations as a compass for navigating the complexities of narcissistic relationships and fostering resilience and empowerment amidst adversity.

5. The author advocates for tools like list-making and intentional engagement with relationship dynamics to validate experiences, counter euphoric recall, and encourage self-care and empowerment.

5. The book emphasizes refraining from futile attempts to communicate with narcissistic individuals, prioritizing emotional well-being and fostering acknowledgment and release.

7. The author underscores the significance of documenting harmful patterns and experiences through lists, validating individuals' experiences, and encouraging self-care and empowerment.

8. The book acknowledges rumination as a significant challenge and encourages embracing it through expression to facilitate healing and release from its hold on the mind.

9. The author highlights extending radical acceptance to oneself as crucial, cultivating self-compassion, resilience, and self-awareness for profound healing and personal transformation.

10. The book concludes with the recognition that radical acceptance is a transformative journey, empowering individuals to reclaim agency over their lives and begin the process of healing.

REFLECTION QUESTIONS

What moments in your relationships trigger discomfort or unease, indicating potential toxicity or imbalance?

Have you ever felt conflicted about maintaining relationships that drain your energy or undermine your self-worth?

How do you cope with the challenges of setting boundaries in relationships, especially with individuals who exhibit narcissistic behavior?

What strategies do you employ to prioritize self-care and emotional well-being amidst the complexities of challenging relationships?

In what ways do you practice self-compassion and self-acceptance when navigating difficult dynamics with others, including those with narcissistic traits?

MILESTONE GOALS

- Readers need to identify and acknowledge toxic patterns in their relationships especially those involving narcissistic behavior, to cultivate awareness and promote healthier interactions.

- Another goal is for readers to develop practical strategies for setting and maintaining boundaries in relationships, prioritizing their emotional well-being and fostering radical acceptance of unchangeable circumstances.

- Readers also aim to explore methods for coping with the aftermath of leaving narcissistic relationships, including managing hoovering attempts, navigating smear campaigns, and embracing the journey of healing and self-discovery.

ACTIONABLE MOVEMENTS

1. **Set Boundaries with Family:** Have an open conversation with family member about setting boundaries to protect your emotional well-being and limit exposure to toxic dynamics.

2. **Join a Support Group:** Explore local or online support groups for individuals navigating narcissistic relationships to share experiences, gain insights, and receive validation from others.

3. **Practice Mindful Communication:** Implement mindful communication techniques when interacting with narcissistic individuals, focusing on clarity, assertiveness, and maintaining personal integrity.

4. **Create a Safe Space:** Designate a physical or virtual space where you can freely express your thoughts, emotions, and experiences without fear of judgment or invalidation.

5. **Engage in Self-Care Rituals:** Establish a self-care routine that includes activities like spending time in nature to rejuvenate your mind, body, and spirit.

6. **Journaling for Reflection:** Start a journal to reflect on your experiences, identify recurring patterns, and gain insights into your emotional responses and coping mechanisms.

7. **Limit Social Media Exposure:** Evaluate your social media usage and consider unfollowing or muting accounts contributing to feelings of inadequacy, comparison, or negativity.

8. **Seek Professional Guidance:** Schedule sessions with a therapist or counselor specializing in narcissistic abuse to process emotions, explore coping strategies, and receive personalized support.

9. **Educate Yourself:** Invest time in learning about narcissistic behavior, trauma recovery, and healthy relationship dynamics through books, articles, podcasts, or workshops to empower yourself with knowledge and understanding.

In the empty pages ahead, you can explore this chapter more deeply and make it your own. Take this opportunity to write your thoughts, ideas, and questions about what you've read so far. Feel free to brainstorm, draw, or note down any questions that pop into your head.

CHAPTER 6:
GRIEF AND HEALING FROM NARCISSISTIC RELATIONSHIPS

Summary

In navigating the complexities of grief and healing from narcissistic relationships individuals often find themselves entangled in a web of emotional turmoil and self-doubt. The journey toward healing involves confronting deep-seated pain acknowledging losses, and rediscovering one's sense of self-worth amidst the wreckage of manipulation and emotional abuse. Through the stories of Maria, Lauren and others, the author illuminates the profound impact of narcissistic relationships on personal identity, emotional well-being, and the grieving process. These narrative serve as poignant reminders of the resilience inherent in the human spirit and the transformative power of self-awareness and empathy in the face of adversity.

Maria's tumultuous relationship with her mother, Clare, epitomizes the intricat dynamics of narcissistic abuse. Clare's volatile behavior, manipulative tendencies, and relentless pursuit of validation cast a shadow over Maria's sense of self-worth from an early age. Despite Maria's efforts to meet her mother's demands and alleviate her insecurities, she finds herself trapped in a cycle of guilt, fear, and emotional turmoil The author uses Maria's narrative to underscore the profound toll of narcissistic parenting on individual growth, emotional resilience, and interpersonal relationship Maria's journey serves as a testament to the enduring legacy of childhood trauma and the formidable obstacles survivors must overcome in their quest for healing and self actualization.

The Narcissistic Relationship: A Dance of Projection and Self-Blame

The author delves into the intricate dynamics of narcissistic relationships, highlighting the cycle of projection, self-blame, and emotional manipulation that characterizes these toxic interactions. Narcissistic individuals weaponize their insecurities and vulnerabilities, projecting them onto their victims in a relentless quest for control and validation. As empathic and accountable individuals, survivors often internalize this toxic dynamic, blaming themselves for the dysfunction and emotional turmoil within the relationship. By elucidating the mechanisms through which narcissistic individuals impose their insecurities onto others, the author sheds light on the enduring impact of emotional abuse and psychological coercion. Understanding these dynamics is crucial for survivors as they navigate the complexities of grief and healing in the aftermath of narcissistic abuse.

Navigating Grief after Narcissistic Abuse: Lauren's Story

Lauren's journey toward healing provides a poignant illustration of the multifaceted nature of grief following narcissistic abuse. Raised in the shadow of a malignant narcissistic father, Lauren grapples with profound feelings of loss, regret, and unfulfilled potential. Her narrative underscores the pervasive influence of narcissistic dynamics on personal relationships, life choices, and emotional well-being. Despite her resilience and determination to break free from the cycle of abuse, Lauren confronts the daunting challenge of rebuilding her sense of self-worth and reclaiming agency over her life. Her journey serves as a beacon of hope for survivors navigating the tumultuous waters of grief and healing, forging a path toward self-discovery, empowerment, and renewed purpose.

The Complexity of Grief in Narcissistic Relationships

Through Lauren's experiences and reflections, the author explores the nuanced layers of grief inherent in narcissistic relationships. From the loss of childhood innocence to the erosion of self-esteem and relational trust, individuals navigate a labyrinth of emotions as they confront the aftermath of narcissistic abuse. The author emphasizes acknowledging and validating these complex grief experiences, even without societal recognition or support. By honoring their pain, survivors pave the way for transformative growth and emotional liberation, reclaiming their voice and agency. Through empathy, self-compassion, and community support, individuals forge a path toward healing, empowerment, and renewed self-discovery in the aftermath of narcissistic abuse.

Grieving the Death of a Narcissistic Person in Your Life

The author delves into the complex emotions that arise following the death of a narcissistic individual, shedding light on the conflicting feelings of relief, guilt, and regret experienced by survivors. Despite the finality of death, the lingering echoes of narcissistic abuse continue to reverberate within survivors, underscoring the enduring nature of emotional trauma and unresolved grievances. By acknowledging the profound impact of narcissistic dynamics on the grieving process, individuals can embark on a journey of self-discovery and emotional liberation, navigating the complexities of grief with courage and resilience.

Blocks to Grieving
In exploring the barriers to grieving, the author highlights common behaviors and coping mechanisms that impede the healing process. From distraction and denial to self-blame and substance abuse, survivors often grapple with a myriad of challenge as they confront the painful realities of narcissistic abuse. By fostering awareness and mindfulness, individuals can transcend these obstacles, embracing the transformative power of vulnerability and self-compassion in their journey toward healing and self renewal.

Navigating Your Grief
The author delineates key strategies for navigating the intricate landscape of narcissistic grief, emphasizing the importance of self-awareness, emotional attunement, and mindful engagement with the grieving process. From naming and honoring one's grief to fostering self-care and personal growth, survivors are empowered to reclaim agency over their narratives and cultivate resilience in adversity. By embracing the tenets of narcissistic grief recovery, individuals forge a path toward self-discovery empowerment, and holistic well-being.

Recovering from the Lie
Through the lens of betrayal and self-doubt, the author explores the multifaceted nature of narcissistic grief, inviting survivors to confront the distorted narratives and painful realities of their past experiences. By dismantling the illusions of trust and authenticity, individuals can cultivate self-compassion and resilience, embracing the complexities of their grief journey with courage and introspection. Through introspection and self-reflection, survivors navigate the tumultuous terrain of narcissistic grief, reclaiming their truth and reclaiming their truth and forging a path toward emotional liberation and healing.

Grieving the Injustice
In confronting the profound injustice of narcissistic relationships, survivors confront the enduring legacy of emotional trauma and unresolved grievances. By embracing radical acceptance and self-compassion, individuals transcend the limitations of blame and resentment, embracing a path of healing and reconciliation. Through the transformative power of self-awareness and empathy, survivors navigate the complexities of narcissistic grief, reclaiming agency over their narratives and fostering a sense of closure and resolution.

The Importance of Therapy in Processing Grief
The author underscores the invaluable role of therapy in navigating the complexities of narcissistic grief, providing survivors with a safe and supportive space to process their emotions and reclaim agency over their narratives. By fostering a culture of

empathy and validation, therapists empower survivors to confront the complexities of their grief journey, promoting resilience and emotional well-being. Through the transformative power of therapeutic intervention, survivors navigate the tumultuous terrain of narcissistic grief, forging a path toward healing, empowerment, and self-discovery.

Grief Rituals

In exploring the significance of grief rituals, survivors reclaim agency over their narratives and foster a sense of closure and resolution. By embracing intentionality and mindfulness, individuals cultivate resilience and emotional well-being, fostering a sense of closure and resolution in the aftermath of narcissistic abuse. Through the transformative power of ritual and reflection, survivors honor the complexities of their grief journey, embracing healing and self-discovery with courage and resilience.

In navigating the complexities of narcissistic grief, survivors embark on a transformative journey of self-discovery and emotional liberation. Through courage, resilience, and self-compassion, individuals reclaim agency over their narratives, fostering healing and reconciliation in the aftermath of narcissistic abuse. By embracing the transformative power of vulnerability and self-awareness, survivors forge a path toward holistic well-being, empowering themselves to embrace the fullness of their truth and reclaim agency over their narratives. As they navigate the complexities of narcissistic grief, survivors embody the resilience and strength inherent in the human spirit, forging a path toward healing, empowerment, and self-discovery.

LESSONS AND KEY POINTS FROM THIS CHAPTER

- The author delves into Maria's struggle with a narcissistic mother, highlighting the profound impact of childhood trauma on self-worth and interpersonal relationships.

- Understanding the complex dynamics of narcissistic relationships, survivors navigate the cycle of projection and self-blame to reclaim agency over their narratives.

- Lauren's journey underscores the multifaceted nature of grief after narcissistic abuse, emphasizing resilience and self-discovery amidst emotional turmoil.

- Survivors confront the enduring legacy of emotional trauma and unresolved grievances, navigating the complexities of grief and healing with courage and resilience.

- The author explores the conflicted emotions following the death of a narcissistic individual, urging survivors to acknowledge their grief and reclaim agency over their narratives.

6. By identifying common blocks to grieving, survivors transcend distractions and self-blame, fostering awareness and self-compassion in their healing journey.

7. Essential strategies for navigating narcissistic grief include self-awareness, emotional attunement, and mindfulness in honoring one's pain and fostering personal growth.

8. Survivors dismantle the illusions of trust and authenticity, reclaiming their truth amidst betrayal and self-doubt and forging a path toward emotional liberation and healing.

REFLECTION QUESTIONS

Have you ever been in a relationship where you felt constantly criticized or devalued? How did this make you think, and what steps did you take to address the situation?

Do you often blame yourself for problems or conflicts in your relationships, even when you know you're not at fault? How does this self-blame affect your emotional well-being?

Have you ever experienced a sense of relief after ending a challenging relationship, even if it brought feelings of guilt or shame? How did you navigate these conflicting emotions?

What are some coping mechanisms you use to deal with the pain and trauma caused by narcissistic abuse? Do these strategies help you in your healing journey, or do they sometimes hinder your progress?

Reflecting on your past experiences, do you believe that justice is essential for healing from narcissistic relationships? How do you define justice in this context, and how does it contribute to your sense of closure and resolution?

MILESTONE GOALS

Readers need to recognize the signs and dynamics of narcissistic relationships to identify and address toxic patterns in their own lives, fostering healthier and more fulfilling interpersonal connections.

Readers need to develop effective coping strategies and self-care practices to navigate the complexities of grief and healing following narcissistic abuse, promoting emotional resilience and well-being.

Readers need to cultivate a deeper understanding of justice and closure in the context of narcissistic relationships, empowering themselves to reclaim agency over their narratives and forge a path toward healing and reconciliation

ACTIONABLE MOVEMENTS

Self-Reflection and Awareness: Begin by reflecting on personal experiences and relationships to identify patterns of narcissistic behavior and emotional abuse. Cultivate self-awareness to recognize how these dynamics impact emotional well-being and interpersonal connections.

Establish Boundaries: Take proactive steps to establish and enforce healthy boundaries in relationships, particularly with individuals who exhibit narcissistic traits. Practice assertiveness and self-advocacy to protect emotional boundaries and promote mutual respect.

3. **Seek Support**: Reach out to trusted friends, family members, or mental health professionals for support and validation. Join support groups or online communities to connect with others who have experienced narcissistic abuse, fostering a sense of solidarity and understanding.

4. **Engage in Therapeutic Practices:** Consider seeking therapy or counseling to explore and process emotions related to narcissistic grief and healing. Work with a qualified therapist to develop coping strategies, build resilience, and cultivate self-compassion in navigating the complexities of grief and recovery.

5. **Practice Self-Care:** Prioritize self-care practices that nurture physical, emotional well-being. Engage in mindfulness meditation, journaling, creative expression, or exercise to promote emotional regulation and stress management.

6. **Educate Yourself:** Take proactive steps to educate yourself about narcissistic personality disorder, emotional abuse dynamics, and strategies for healing and recovery. Utilize reputable resources such as books, articles, and workshops to deepen understanding and cultivate empowerment.

7. **Embrace Forgiveness and Closure:** Explore forgiveness as a tool for releasing resentment and reclaiming personal power in the aftermath of narcissistic abuse. Practice forgiveness towards oneself and others, acknowledging that closure is a process rather than a destination.

8. **Celebrate Progress:** Acknowledge and celebrate small victories and milestones along the healing journey from narcissistic relationships. Cultivate a sense of resilience and self-compassion by recognizing the courage and strength it takes to confront adversity and pursue personal growth.

In the empty pages ahead, you can explore this chapter more deeply and make it your own. Take this opportunity to write your thoughts, ideas, and questions about what you've read so far. Feel free to brainstorm, draw, or note down any questions that pop into your head.

CHAPTER 7: BECOME MORE NARCISSIST RESISTANT

Summary

In the journey of personal growth and healing, individuals often encounter challenge stemming from narcissistic relationships. Through the narrative of individuals lik Lin and Celine, the author explores the intricate dynamics of narcissistic abuse resilience, and the quest for self-discovery. In this exploration, the author delves int the nuanced aspects of healing from narcissistic trauma and developing resilienc against gaslighting tactics. By examining the stories of Lin and Celine, readers ar invited to delve deeper into the complexities of navigating relationships marked b manipulation, toxicity, and the enduring quest for self-empowerment.

The author uses the story of Lin, who endured narcissistic relationships, to underscor the arduous path of healing from narcissistic abuse. Lin's journey of setting boundarie seeking therapy, and confronting toxic dynamics highlights the transformative powe of resilience and self-discovery. By embracing healthier boundaries and recognizin narcissistic patterns, individuals like Lin embark on a journey of psychologica empowerment and self-reclamation. Through Lin's narrative, readers witness th evolution of self-awareness and the courage required to break free from the shackle of narcissistic manipulation.

The Persistence of Narcissistic Patterns
Despite efforts to heal, individuals like Lin often grapple with the fear of reencounterin narcissistic personalities. The author emphasizes the pervasive nature of narcissisti behaviors and the challenges of identifying and managing toxic relationship

Through introspection and discernment, individuals cultivate the psychological fortitude needed to navigate future encounters with narcissistic individuals. By acknowledging the ubiquity of narcissistic patterns in various spheres of life, readers are encouraged to remain vigilant and resilient in the face of potential adversity.

Becoming Narcissist Resistant

Transitioning to a state of narcissist resistance requires a multifaceted approach rooted in self-awareness and empowerment. By fostering discernment, setting boundaries, and embracing radical acceptance, individuals equip themselves with the tools to resist manipulation and gaslighting tactics. The author provides insights into recognizing early signs of narcissism, navigating different phases of relationships, and reclaiming autonomy in the face of manipulation. Through proactive strategies and a commitment to self-empowerment, individuals cultivate resilience and assertiveness in their interactions with narcissistic individuals.

Resisting Gaslighting Tactics

Through the narrative of Celine's experiences, the author explores the insidious nature of gaslighting within narcissistic relationships. Gaslighting, characterized by the denial of reality and manipulation of perception, undermines individuals' sense of self and autonomy. By fostering self-trust, validating subjective experiences, and disengaging from gaslighting dynamics, individuals cultivate resilience against manipulation and reclaim agency over their narratives. Through Celine's journey, readers gain insight into the psychological toll of gaslighting and the importance of maintaining clarity and self-assurance amidst manipulation attempts.

Cultivating Self-Validation

Central to narcissist resistance is the cultivation of self-validation and mindfulness. By reconnecting with one's subjective reality, individuals challenge gaslighting narratives and reclaim ownership of their experiences. Through journaling, self-reflection, and seeking supportive spaces, individuals foster resilience and fortify themselves against the psychological toll of narcissistic relationships. The author emphasizes the importance of nurturing healthy relationships and creating gaslight-free zones where individuals feel validated, accepted, and empowered. Through intentional practices and a commitment to self-empowerment, individuals embark on a journey of self-discovery and resilience amidst the complexities of narcissistic abuse.

Your Inner Critic Is Trying to Tell You Something

The author suggests that your inner critic isn't just a random bug in your brain but rather a part of you trying to shield you from failure or hurt, albeit in a harsh way. For instance, if you listen to your inner critic and don't apply for a job, you might avoid the pain of rejection. However, the author uses the story of individuals like Lin to show that your inner critic can become more like an inner tormentor, making you feel worthless. By recognizing its role as a misguided protector, you can stop seeing it as your identity and understand it as an attempt to avoid more pain. Communicating with your inner critic, even out loud, can help reframe its voice as a means of self protection in narcissistic relationships.

Understanding Your Sympathetic Nervous System
Christina's experiences illustrate how the fallout of narcissistic abuse can manifest physically. Her body reacted to her wife's behavior and later to her colleague's actions, almost like an early warning system. The author explains that the sympathetic nervous system (SNS) governs these physical responses to fear and threat, activating fight, flight, freeze, and fawn/submit responses. These reactions, involuntary and reflexive, are not always helpful in narcissistic relationships. Flight, for example, can involve distancing yourself emotionally or mentally from the relationship. Freeze and fawn responses also reflect attempts to cope with threat or danger.

Learning to Manage Your SNS
Living through narcissistic abuse can leave you in a constant state of tension, even after the relationship ends. Chronic arousal from the sympathetic nervous system can lead to harmful survivor patterns like walking on eggshells or feeling constantly distracted. To counteract this, the author advises tapping into the parasympathetic nervous system (PNS), which governs relaxation and rest. Stress management techniques such as deep breathing, and establishing bedtime routines can help regulate the body's stress response. Understanding and connecting with your body's reactions can also help manage SNS responses during triggering situations.

How Can I Support Someone Experiencing Narcissistic Abuse?
Supporting someone healing from narcissistic abuse requires empathy and understanding. Instead of labeling the abuser as narcissistic, the author suggests offering non-judgmental support and encouraging therapy. Sharing memories of happier times or reminding the person of their skills and joys can help them open up. Additionally, asking them directly what they need—help, a listening ear, or hug—can provide valuable support without judgment or pressure. Being there for someone healing from narcissistic abuse can facilitate their recovery journey while also fostering your healing process.

Building Resistance
The author delves into strategies for resisting narcissistic individuals and safeguarding oneself from toxic relationships. Individuals gain insight into their emotional reactions by recognizing gaslighting and sympathetic nervous system responses. The author emphasizes cultivating self-awareness and connecting with one's inner voice amidst manipulative dynamics.

Go No Contact
Drawing from real-life experiences, the author highlights the efficacy of implementing a no-contact strategy to break free from toxic cycles. Individuals assert their autonomy and protect themselves from further manipulation by ceasing communication and

etting firm boundaries. The author acknowledges the challenges of maintaining no contact, especially in familial or professional settings. Despite the discomfort and potential backlash, no connection is vital for reclaiming personal agency and fostering emotional well-being.

When You Have to Break No Contact

Navigating the complexities of breaking no contact requires introspection and flexibility. The author underscores the need to prioritize personal well-being while acknowledging external pressures and familial obligations. By reframing perceptions of loyalty and embracing circumspection, individuals navigate the delicate balance between self-preservation and familial ties. The author encourages individuals to honor their emotional boundaries while remaining open to reconciliation under appropriate circumstances.

Firewalling

The concept of firewalling, borrowed from the realm of technology, offers a metaphorical framework for establishing emotional boundaries. Individuals protect themselves from manipulation and exploitation by safeguarding against emotional "malware" and exercising discernment in interpersonal interactions. The author emphasizes the importance of moving cautiously in new relationships and refraining from divulging sensitive information prematurely. Through mindful discernment and self-protective measures, individuals cultivate resilience against narcissistic influences.

Gatekeeping

Embracing a proactive approach to self-care, individuals prioritize their emotional well-being by limiting exposure to toxic environments and individuals. The author underscores the liberating effect of asserting boundaries and declining invitations that jeopardize emotional health. Individuals reclaim agency over their social interactions and environments by embracing self-advocacy and prioritizing personal integrity. Gatekeeping is a powerful tool for fostering emotional resilience and nurturing authentic connections.

Understanding the Enablers

To fortify resilience against narcissistic dynamics, individuals must recognize the role of enablers in perpetuating toxic relationships. The author highlights the insidious influence of individuals who excuse or minimize narcissistic behavior, perpetuating cycles of manipulation and gaslighting. Individuals mitigate self-doubt and assert their reality in the face of external invalidation by cultivating awareness of enabler dynamics and trusting personal instincts. Understanding the psychology of enablers empowers individuals to break free from toxic relationships and prioritize self-validation.

The Twelve-Month Cleanse

Embarking on a period of self-imposed solitude, individuals undergo a transformative journey of self-discovery and healing. The author advocates for a year-long cleanse to recalibrate personal identity and foster independence from past trauma bonds. By embracing solitude and nurturing individual interests, individuals reclaim autonomy and rediscover personal agency. The cleanse serves as a pivotal period for introspection, growth, and the cultivation of resilience against future narcissistic influences.

The Power of Solitude

Finding solace in solitude, individuals embark on self-reclamation and emotional renewal. The author underscores the importance of embracing solitude as a healing space for self-reflection and personal growth. By challenging societal stigma surrounding loneliness and embracing solitude as a source of strength, individuals dismantle toxic narratives and reclaim ownership of their emotional narratives. Solitude becomes a sanctuary for self-discovery and empowerment, enabling individuals to cultivate resilience and authenticity in their relationships.

Be Okay with Good Enough

Rejecting perfectionism, individuals embrace a mindset of self-compassion and acceptance. The author advocates prioritizing self-care and acknowledging personal limitations in pursuing emotional well-being. By reframing expectations and embracing imperfection, individuals alleviate self-imposed pressure and foster sense of inner peace. Embracing the principle of "good enough" serves as a catalyst for healing and self-acceptance amidst the complexities of narcissistic abuse.

Embrace Joy

Amidst the tumult of narcissistic relationships, individuals reclaim joy as an act of defiance and self-preservation. The author encourages individuals to savor moments of happiness and cultivate gratitude for life's simple pleasures. By prioritizing personal well-being and embracing moments of joy, individuals disrupt patterns of emotional deprivation and reclaim agency over their emotional narratives. Happiness becomes a beacon of resilience and hope, guiding individuals toward emotional liberation and authentic self-expression.

Narcissist resistance is a journey of self-discovery, healing, and empowerment. By embracing resilience strategies and prioritizing emotional well-being, individuals reclaim agency over their lives and navigate narcissistic dynamics with greater discernment and authenticity. Through self-awareness and the cultivation of joy, individuals forge a path toward emotional liberation and authentic self-expression in the face of adversity.

LESSONS AND KEY POINTS FROM THIS CHAPTER

- The author illustrates the transformative journey of healing from narcissistic abuse through narratives like Lin's, emphasizing the importance of setting boundaries, seeking therapy, and confronting toxic dynamics to reclaim self-empowerment and resilience.

- Despite efforts to heal, individuals like Lin often confront the enduring presence of narcissistic behaviors, necessitating vigilance, and discernment in navigating future relationships and encounters with manipulative individuals, as the book highlights.

- The book advocates for proactive strategies rooted in self-awareness and empowerment, enabling individuals to resist manipulation, set boundaries, and reclaim autonomy in interactions with narcissistic individuals, fostering resilience and assertiveness.

- By recognizing the insidious nature of gaslighting and fostering self-trust and validation, individuals cultivate resilience against manipulation, reclaiming agency over their narratives amidst gaslighting dynamics, as detailed by the author.

- The book advocates for nurturing self-validation to challenge gaslighting narratives, fostering resilience and fortitude against the psychological toll of narcissistic relationships, the author emphasizes.

- The author reframes the inner critic as a misguided protector rather than an identity, enabling individuals to communicate with it to mitigate its negative impact and navigate narcissistic relationships more effectively.

- Recognizing the physical manifestations of narcissistic abuse through the sympathetic nervous system's responses enables individuals to manage stress and arousal effectively, as outlined in the book.

- Employing stress management techniques and connecting with the parasympathetic nervous system facilitates the regulation of stress responses and promotes emotional well-being in the aftermath of narcissistic abuse, according to the book's insights.

- Offering non-judgmental support, encouraging therapy, and validating experiences can facilitate healing for individuals navigating narcissistic abuse, fostering empathy and understanding in the support process, as the book suggests.

10. Through strategies like going no contact, firewalling, and gatekeeping, individuals safeguard themselves from toxic relationships, cultivate self-awareness, and assert boundaries, fostering resilience and empowerment in the face of narcissistic dynamics, as detailed in the book.

REFLECTION QUESTIONS

Have you ever questioned the intentions or sincerity of someone in your life especially after feeling manipulated or invalidated?

How do you cope with feelings of self-doubt or worthlessness, especially in relationships where your experiences are dismissed or distorted?

What strategies do you employ to maintain emotional balance and resilience when faced with criticism or gaslighting from others?

Can you identify times when your inner critic has hindered your progress or self esteem, and how have you responded to its negative messages?

n what ways do you prioritize your emotional well-being and set boundaries o protect yourself from toxic dynamics, both in personal and professional relationships?

MILESTONE GOALS

Readers need to recognize and validate their own experiences of narcissistic abuse or manipulation, fostering a sense of self-awareness and empowerment in navigating future relationships.

Readers must develop strategies for setting and enforcing healthy boundaries in their interactions, prioritizing their emotional well-being and resilience against gaslighting tactics.

Readers need to cultivate a supportive network of friends, family, or professionals who understand and validate their experiences, fostering a sense of community and empowerment in their journey toward narcissist resistance and healing.

ACTIONABLE MOVEMENTS

- **Self-Reflection and Journaling:** Dedicate time each day for self-reflection and journaling to identify patterns of behavior, emotional triggers, and instances of gaslighting or manipulation in your relationships.

- **Seek Therapy or Support Groups:** Take proactive steps to seek therapy or join support groups where you can share experiences, gain validation, and learn coping strategies for dealing with narcissistic abuse.

- **Establish Clear Boundaries:** Identify areas where you need to establish boundaries in your relationships and communicate them assertively and clearly to others. Practice saying "no" when necessary and prioritize your emotional well-being.

- **Practice Mindfulness and Stress Management:** Incorporate mindfulness techniques such as meditation, deep breathing exercises, and yoga into your daily routine to manage stress, regulate emotions, and cultivate inner peace.

5. **Develop a Support Network:** Surround yourself with supportive friends, family members, or support groups who validate your experiences, offer empathy, and provide a safe space for healing and growth.

6. **Implement No-Contact or Limited Contact:** Evaluate your relationships and consider implementing no-contact or limited-contact strategies with toxic individuals who consistently undermine your well-being and boundaries.

7. **Engage in Self-Care Activities:** Prioritize self-care activities that nurture your physical, emotional, and mental well-being, such as exercise, hobbies, spending time in nature, and engaging in activities that bring you joy.

8. **Practice Assertiveness and Self-Validation:** Practice assertive communication techniques to express your needs, feelings, and boundaries confidently without fear of backlash or invalidation. Focus on self-validation and affirmations to reinforce your worth and agency.

9. **Monitor Progress and Adjust Strategies:** Regularly assess your progress in implementing these strategies and be open to adjusting your approach as needed. Celebrate small victories and be compassionate with yourself during setbacks or challenges.

In the empty pages ahead, you can explore this chapter more deeply and make it your own. Take this opportunity to write your thoughts, ideas, and questions about what you've read so far. Feel free to brainstorm, draw, or note down any questions that pop into your head.

CHAPTER 8:
HEAL AND GROW
WHEN YOU STAY

Summary

In this chapter, the author delves into the intricacies of navigating narcissisti relationships while seeking healing and growth. The narrative unfolds through th lens of Pauline's experiences, highlighting individuals' challenges when staying in suc complex dynamics. By examining Pauline's struggles with narcissistic relationships i various aspects of her life, the chapter aims to provide insights and strategies fo maintaining well-being and autonomy amidst adversity.

Pauline serves as a poignant example of the journey towards radical acceptance ami the tumult of narcissistic relationships. While managing the narcissistic dynamic within her family and workplace, Pauline finds solace in fleeting moments of jo and purpose. However, beneath the surface lies a profound sense of grief and env stemming from the inability to engage in meaningful connections fully. Despit her resilience, Pauline grapples with the emotional toll of navigating narcissisti personalities, embodying the complexities inherent in such relationships.

The Dynamics of Staying

The author meticulously unpacks the multifaceted reasons individuals opt to remain i narcissistic relationships, ranging from pragmatic considerations to deeply ingraine cultural pressures. Whether driven by financial dependence, familial obligation or fear of societal judgment, the decision to stay is often fraught with conflictin emotions and ethical dilemmas. Through Pauline's narrative, the chapter underscore the importance of introspection in navigating the intricate web of motivations tha ompel individuals to maintain ties with narcissistic personalities.

Balancing Healing and Staying

Navigating the delicate balance between healing and staying in narcissistic relationships necessitates a nuanced approach rooted in self-awareness and compassion. By delineating the different levels of engagement within such dynamics, the chapter offers practical techniques for preserving one's well-being while remaining tethered to toxic environments. From setting boundaries to cultivating resilience, individuals are encouraged to prioritize their emotional health while navigating the complexities of relational entanglement.

Overcoming Barriers to Healing

Healing within the confines of a narcissistic relationship requires courage, resilience, and a steadfast commitment to self-discovery. Despite the pervasive nature of cognitive dissonance and fear of abandonment, individuals are empowered to confront internalized narratives and reclaim agency over their narratives. Through Pauline's journey, the chapter underscores the transformative power of self-compassion and authenticity in transcending the confines of dysfunctional dynamics and embracing the path toward healing.

Navigating Love and Attachment

Acknowledging the enduring presence of love and attachment amidst the tumult of narcissistic relationships, the chapter invites individuals to embrace the complexity of their emotions without judgment or self-recrimination. By honoring the intricacies of trauma bonds and relational dynamics, individuals can cultivate a deeper understanding of their own experiences while forging a path toward inner reconciliation and emotional liberation.

Understanding the Impact of Staying

While acknowledging the inherent challenges and limitations of remaining in narcissistic relationships, the chapter emphasizes the importance of cultivating awareness and setting realistic expectations. By recognizing the toll of prolonged exposure to toxic dynamics, individuals are empowered to prioritize their well-being and pursue avenues of healing and growth. Through resilience, self-compassion, and unwavering self-awareness, individuals can navigate the complexities of staying in narcissistic relationships while fostering a sense of inner resilience and empowerment.

Depleted Bandwidth

When grappling with the reality of narcissistic behavior, individuals often find themselves entangled in its repercussions. These may range from strained relationships with loved ones to thwarted personal ambitions, depleting their emotional reserves. The scarcity of compassion and respect exacerbates this depletion, hindering personal growth and fostering burnout. Realistic self-care becomes paramount in such circumstances. It involves recognizing signs of emotional fatigue, such as persistent self-doubt or physical exhaustion, and responding accordingly. By addressing emotional scarcity and seeking out empathetic environments, individual can gradually replenish their resilience, empowering themselves to navigate toxi relationships with greater fortitude.

Not Feeling Like the Same Person

Living in proximity to a narcissist can profoundly distort one's self-perception. often leads to feelings of envy towards individuals leading more harmonious lives emotional numbness, or even harboring uncharacteristically mean thoughts. The recognition of these tumultuous emotions is a crucial step in reclaiming one's self concept from the shadows of narcissistic influence. By embracing the complexity of their feelings and practicing self-compassion, individuals can begin to reconcile the dissonance between their authentic selves and the personas they adopt in narcissisti environments.

Being Mean to Yourself

The decision to remain in a narcissistic relationship often fosters an environment of self-devaluation. Individuals may find themselves engaging in relentless self-criticism mirroring the disparaging treatment they receive from the narcissist. Overcoming thi self-perpetuating cycle requires a conscious effort to cultivate self-compassion. By envisioning and nurturing their inner child, individuals can confront the origins of their self-deprecation and gradually replace it with self-nurturance. This process of self-reclamation is pivotal in breaking free from the toxic dynamics that underpi narcissistic relationships.

How Do You Stay?

In navigating the complexities of narcissistic relationships, setting and enforcin boundaries emerge as indispensable tools for self-preservation. However, the proces of boundary-setting can evoke deep-seated fears and insecurities. It necessitate a compassionate exploration of one's boundaries and a steadfast commitmer to self-kindness. By asserting boundaries and prioritizing emotional well-bein and autonomy, individuals can reclaim agency within toxic dynamics and foste environments conducive to personal growth.

Low Contact

Maintaining low contact with narcissistic individuals serves as a pragmatic strateg for minimizing emotional entanglement while preserving familial ties. Individual can navigate familial dynamics with autonomy and resilience by setting clear limit on interactions and prioritizing emotional well-being. However, establishing health boundaries requires deliberate engagement and a steadfast commitment to sel preservation.

Gray Rock and Yellow Rock

The techniques of gray rocking and yellow rocking offer nuanced approaches to managing communication with narcissistic individuals. Gray rocking, characterized by emotional detachment, protects against manipulation and emotional turmoil. Conversely, yellow rocking infuses interactions with warmth and politeness, allowing individuals to maintain authenticity while mitigating conflict. By adopting these strategies, individuals can assert boundaries, preserve personal integrity, and navigate narcissistic relationships with greater resilience and self-assurance.

Don't Go DEEP!

The author illustrates the challenges of communicating with narcissistic individuals through Callie's experience with her demanding brother. The DEEP technique is a practical tool for avoiding toxic interactions by refraining from Defending, Engaging, Explaining, and Personalizing. By recognizing the futility of defending oneself and the manipulative nature of explanations, individuals can safeguard their emotional well-being and refrain from being drawn into futile arguments and gaslighting.

Stop Making It About Them

Remaining in narcissistic relationships often leads individuals to tether their sense of self-worth to the narcissist's perceptions. However, healing necessitates disengaging from the narcissistic person's narrative and prioritizing personal growth and happiness independently of their influence. By detaching from the need for validation or retaliation, individuals can reclaim agency over their narratives and foster emotional liberation from the constraints of the narcissistic relationship.

Address the Self-Blame

The author emphasizes the importance of recognizing and addressing patterns of self-blame that perpetuate the cycle of emotional turmoil within narcissistic relationships. Individuals can confront underlying feelings of shame and guilt through self-monitoring and open dialogue with trusted confidants. By documenting and analyzing interactions that reinforce self-blame, individuals gain insight into their thought patterns and empower themselves to break free from harmful cycles of validation-seeking behavior.

Find Your True North

Identifying and prioritizing one's "True North"—family, personal beliefs, or core values—is a guiding principle for navigating interactions with narcissistic individuals. By discerning between meaningful battles worth engaging in and futile conflicts, individuals can conserve their emotional energy and assert boundaries without succumbing to manipulation or gaslighting. However, individuals must remain vigilant against attempts to exploit their vulnerabilities and reevaluate the relationship dynamics accordingly.

Prepare and Release

Preparation and decompression strategies enable individuals to navigate interaction with narcissistic individuals with resilience and self-assurance. By allowing time for emotional recalibration after challenging interactions, individuals can mitigate the impact of psychological stress and foster emotional resilience. These rituals serve as vital tools for maintaining equilibrium and promoting psychological well-being amidst the tumult of narcissistic relationships.

Never Call Them Out as a Narcissist

The author advises against confronting narcissistic individuals about their personality traits, as such confrontations often escalate conflict and yield little resolution. Instead, individuals are encouraged to focus on their healing journey and refrain from seeking validation or acknowledgment from the narcissist. By refraining from engaging in futile attempts to change the narcissist, individuals can redirect their energy toward personal growth and emotional well-being, independent of the narcissist's influence.

Get Therapy and Support

The author emphasizes the critical role of therapy for individuals entangled in narcissistic relationships. Therapy serves as a vital resource for navigating the complexities of narcissistic abuse and provides a supportive space for processing emotions and experiences. While therapy may not offer quick fixes, it is a cornerstone for promoting mental well-being and resilience. The chapter underscores the importance of accessible and affordable mental health services, recognizing the barriers faced by individuals with limited resources.

Soul Distancing

Soul distancing offers a strategy for preserving one's emotional well-being while remaining in a narcissistic relationship. Drawing from personal anecdotes, the author illustrates the importance of safeguarding one's vulnerabilities and aspirations from invalidating behavior. By establishing emotional boundaries and reframing interactions with narcissistic individuals, individuals can mitigate the detrimental effects of relational toxicity. Soul distancing empowers individuals to prioritize their inner peace and authenticity amidst challenging circumstances.

Leaving a narcissistic relationship or disengaging from a narcissistic person may not always be feasible. However, the chapter asserts that healing and personal growth remain attainable goals, even within the confines of such relationships. By leveraging therapeutic support, cultivating resilience, and practicing soul distancing, individuals can navigate the complexities of narcissistic dynamics while reclaiming agency over their lives. Healing is a personal and transformative process marked by small calibrations and shifts toward self-empowerment and authenticity.

LESSONS AND KEY POINTS FROM THIS CHAPTER

- The chapter emphasizes the intricacies of navigating narcissistic relationships, offering insights into maintaining well-being and autonomy amidst adversity.

- Pauline's narrative exemplifies radical acceptance amid narcissistic dynamics, underscoring the complexities inherent in such relationships and the toll they take on individuals.

- Staying in narcissistic relationships involves nuanced motivations, from pragmatic considerations to cultural pressures, demanding introspection.

- Balancing healing and staying necessitates setting boundaries and prioritizing emotional health within toxic environments, fostering resilience and self-awareness.

- Overcoming barriers to healing involves confronting internalized narratives and reclaiming agency over personal narratives, fostering self-compassion and authenticity.

- Acknowledging enduring love and attachment amidst narcissistic relationships invites embracing complexity without judgment, fostering inner reconciliation and emotional liberation.

- Understanding the impact of staying underscores the importance of awareness and realistic expectations, empowering individuals to prioritize well-being and pursue healing and growth.

- Techniques like soul distancing and therapy offer strategies for preserving emotional well-being and navigating relational toxicity, empowering individuals to reclaim agency and authenticity.

REFLECTION QUESTIONS

How do you recognize signs of toxicity in your relationships, and what steps do you take to protect your emotional well-being?

Have you ever felt pressured to stay in a relationship or maintain contact with someone toxic due to societal expectations or personal obligations?

What strategies do you employ to maintain boundaries and preserve your self worth in challenging interpersonal dynamics?

How do you navigate feelings of love and attachment towards individuals who exhibit harmful behavior, such as manipulation or emotional abuse?

In what ways do you prioritize your mental health and seek support, especially when facing difficulties in toxic relationships?

MILESTONE GOALS

- Readers need to understand the intricacies of navigating narcissistic relationships and gain insights into maintaining well-being and autonomy within such dynamics.

- Readers need to identify personal motivations for staying in toxic relationships and develop strategies for setting boundaries and prioritizing emotional health

Readers need to learn practical techniques like soul distancing and seeking therapy to preserve emotional well-being and reclaim agency in challenging relational dynamics.

ACTIONABLE MOVEMENTS

- **Reflect on personal relationships:** Take time to assess the dynamics of your relationships and identify any patterns of toxicity or emotional manipulation.

- **Establish boundaries:** Clearly define your boundaries and communicate them assertively to those in your life, especially individuals who exhibit narcissistic traits.

- **Seek therapy or support groups:** Explore options for therapy or support groups tailored explicitly to survivors of narcissistic abuse to gain insights and coping strategies.

- **Practice self-care:** Prioritize self-care activities such as exercise, and hobbies that promote emotional well-being and resilience.

- **Engage in soul distancing:** Learn to protect your vulnerabilities and aspirations from invalidating behavior by practicing emotional boundaries and reframing interactions with toxic individuals.

- **Educate yourself:** Continuously educate yourself about narcissistic behavior and manipulation tactics to empower yourself in navigating challenging relationships.

- **Cultivate supportive relationships:** Surround yourself with empathetic and understanding individuals who validate your experiences and provide emotional support.

- **Take steps towards healing:** Embrace the journey towards healing by acknowledging your emotions, confronting internalized narratives, and prioritizing your mental health and self-growth.

In the empty pages ahead, you can explore this chapter more deeply and make it your own. Take this opportunity to write your thoughts, ideas, and questions about what you've read so far. Feel free to brainstorm, draw, or note down any questions that pop into your head.

CHAPTER 9:
REWRITE YOUR STORY

Summary

In this chapter, the author uses Luna's tumultuous yet transformative journey throug[h] the labyrinth of narcissistic abuse and personal redemption to serve as a beacon o[f] hope for those navigating similar storms. Her narrative, deeply ingrained with th[e] scars of emotional turmoil and the resilience of the human spirit, illuminates th[e] complexities of healing, self-discovery, and the pursuit of authentic fulfillment.

Luna's story begins in the crucible of her immigrant family, where the echoes o[f] traditional values and patriarchal norms reverberate through her childhood. As th[e] "hopeful robot," Luna grapples with the suffocating weight of parental expectation[s] and the emotional wreckage wrought by a narcissistic father and a mother trapped i[n] a cycle of abuse. In the shadow of familial dysfunction, Luna emerges as the golde[n] child, burdened with the weight of unrealized dreams and stifled aspirations.

Her journey unfolds against a backdrop of profound emotional complexity as sh[e] navigates the treacherous terrain of toxic relationships and fractured identities. He[r] pursuit of academic excellence and professional success becomes a battleground fo[r] self-worth, marred by the relentless specter of inadequacy and the relentless pursu[it] of external validation.

Navigating Career and Personal Challenges
Despite her academic prowess and professional achievements as a physicia[n] Luna finds herself ensnared in a web of self-doubt and existential uncertaint[y]

The tumultuous landscape of her relationships mirrors the turbulent waters of her professional ambitions as she grapples with the debilitating legacy of childhood trauma and the pervasive influence of societal expectations.

Her journey unfolds as a testament to the resilience of the human spirit as she confronts the demons of her past and embraces the daunting prospect of personal transformation. Through the crucible of adversity, Luna discovers the latent reservoirs of strength and resilience within herself, embarking on a journey of self-discovery and empowerment that defies the shackles of her past.

Embracing Healing and Personal Growth

In the crucible of healing, Luna confronts the pervasive legacy of narcissistic abuse and embarks on a journey of profound self-discovery and personal transformation. Through the cathartic embrace of therapy and introspection, she unearths the buried fragments of her fractured identity and confronts the shadows of her past with unwavering courage and resilience.

Her decision to sever the shackles of toxic relationships and reclaim her autonomy marks a pivotal moment in her journey toward self-realization and emotional liberation. Despite the daunting specter of financial uncertainty and emotional upheaval, Luna emerges from the crucible of adversity with newfound clarity and purpose, embracing the boundless potential of her authentic self.

Reflections on Resilience and Hope

Luna's narrative embodies the transformative power of resilience and self-awareness, transcending the confines of trauma and adversity to embrace a future defined by authenticity and hope. Her journey serves as a poignant reminder of the indomitable spirit of the human soul, resilient in the face of life's most significant trials and steadfast in its pursuit of redemption and renewal.

Embracing Posttraumatic Growth and Healing

In the aftermath of trauma and emotional upheaval, Luna's journey toward healing and self-discovery is a beacon of hope for those navigating similar storms. Through the crucible of adversity, she discovers the latent reservoirs of strength and resilience within herself, emerging from the crucible of trauma with newfound clarity and purpose.

Her journey exemplifies the transformative potential of posttraumatic growth as she navigates the labyrinth of healing with unwavering courage and determination. Luna's narrative is a testament to the human capacity for resilience and renewal, transcending the confines of trauma and adversity to embrace a future defined by authenticity, purpose, and hope.

The Tale of the Lion

The author uses Luna's story to illustrate the journey of rewriting one's narrative from the perspective of empowerment and self-discovery. Luna's tale reflects the struggle many individuals face in breaking free from the confines of narcissistic relationships and reclaiming their sense of identity.

Luna's journey highlights the profound impact of narcissistic relationships on one's sense of self. From an early age, she grappled with the suffocating influence of familial expectations and the relentless pursuit of validation from narcissistic figures in her life. Her story underscores the pervasive nature of emotional manipulation and the profound sense of entanglement that defines such relationships.

As Luna embarks on her journey of self-discovery, she confronts the ingrained patterns of behavior shaped by years of narcissistic abuse. The author emphasizes the importance of understanding the impact of these relationships on one's identity and the need to redefine oneself outside the confines of the narcissist's narrative.

Revising Your Narrative

The author underscores the importance of revisiting and revising the narrative shaped by narcissistic relationships. Drawing parallels to rewriting a familiar fairy tale, the author encourages individuals to challenge the distorted perceptions and misassumptions perpetuated by narcissistic abuse.

Through introspection and self-reflection, individuals can identify the underlying narratives that have hindered their personal growth and empowerment. By recognizing the influence of narcissistic dynamics on their beliefs and behaviors, they can begin the process of rewriting their stories from a place of authenticity and self-compassion.

The author emphasizes the need to differentiate between the narratives imposed by narcissistic figures and one's authentic identity. By acknowledging and reframing past experiences through a lens of self-compassion, individuals can reclaim agency over their lives and chart a new course grounded in truth and resilience.

The Treachery of Forgiveness

The author challenges conventional notions of forgiveness within the context of narcissistic relationships. While forgiveness is often heralded as a virtue, the author acknowledges its limitations in the face of repeated harm and manipulation.

Drawing from personal and professional experiences, the author highlights the complexities of forgiveness in narcissistic dynamics. Rather than viewing forgiveness as a prerequisite for healing, the author encourages individuals to prioritize self-compassion and acceptance in their journey toward recovery.

By reframing forgiveness as a choice rather than an obligation, individuals can honor their experiences and prioritize their emotional well-being. The author advocates for a nuanced approach to healing that embraces self-forgiveness and liberation from the narratives of narcissistic abuse.

From Survivor to Thriver

The author illustrates the journey from survivor to thriver after narcissistic abuse, emphasizing the possibility of growth and healing beyond the confines of trauma. Thriving isn't about reverting to the "old you" but embracing a wiser, more self-aware, and authentic self. It involves transcending the daily struggle of survival and finding liberation from the influence of narcissistic figures in one's life. Through numerous survivor stories, the author highlights that thriving can manifest in subtle yet profound shifts in perspective and emotional well-being.

Navigating Closure and Moving Forward

The author delves into the elusive concept of closure in narcissistic relationships, emphasizing that closure may never come in the conventional sense. Waiting for acknowledgment or accountability from the narcissistic individual can lead to a perpetual cycle of disappointment. Instead, closure entails reclaiming one's sense of self and purpose and moving forward despite the absence of resolution. It's about closing the chapter with the narcissistic figure and forging a new narrative centered on personal growth and empowerment.

Activities to Foster Healing and Recovery

A series of therapeutic exercises are presented to facilitate healing and recovery from narcissistic abuse. These exercises challenge distorted narratives, promote autonomy, and cultivate self-compassion. From rewriting childhood fairy tales to reflecting on emotional experiences and writing letters to oneself, each activity encourages introspection and self-reflection. By engaging in these exercises, survivors can gradually reclaim their narrative and embrace their journey toward healing with compassion and resilience.

Embracing Posttraumatic Growth and Healing

The author explores the concept of posttraumatic growth, highlighting the potential for profound transformation and resilience in the aftermath of narcissistic abuse. While the healing journey is fraught with challenges and setbacks, it also offers opportunities for growth, gratitude, and a more profound sense of purpose. By reframing their narrative and embracing self-compassion, survivors can embark on a journey of self-discovery and empowerment, transcending the confines of trauma and reclaiming their authentic selves.

In conclusion, the author underscores the transformative power of healing and self-discovery in the aftermath of narcissistic abuse. By embracing their journey from survivor to thriver, individuals can break free from trauma and forge a path toward resilience, authenticity, and inner peace. While the road to recovery may be arduous and fraught with challenges, it ultimately leads to a renewed sense of self and a life filled with possibility and purpose. Through compassion, introspection, and perseverance, survivors can emerge from their past's shadows and embrace their future selves' boundless potential.

LESSONS AND KEY POINTS FROM THIS CHAPTER

1. The author delineates the complex journey of healing and self-discovery after narcissistic abuse, offering insight into the profound challenges and triumphs.

2. Through introspection, individuals confront the pervasive influence of narcissistic relationships on identity and interpersonal dynamics.

3. Professional success often juxtaposes with personal struggles, highlighting the intricate interplay between external achievements and internal turmoil.

4. Embracing healing entails confronting past traumas and reshaping narrative from a place of authenticity and self-compassion.

5. Resilience and self-awareness emerge as guiding principles, illuminating the path towards redemption and personal fulfilment.

6. The author challenges conventional views on forgiveness, prioritizing self-compassion and acceptance over obligatory forgiveness.

7. Transitioning from survivor to thriver involves navigating closure, embracing growth, and forging new narratives grounded in resilience.

8. Therapeutic activities catalyze healing, encouraging individuals to rewrite distorted narratives and reclaim autonomy.

9. Posttraumatic growth offers a pathway towards resilience and gratitude transcending trauma towards a renewed sense of purpose.

REFLECTION QUESTIONS

Reflecting on your past relationships, do you notice any patterns of behaviour or emotional dynamics that resemble those in narcissistic relationships?

Consider your current narrative about forgiveness. Are there instances where you've felt pressured to forgive someone despite still feeling hurt or resentful?

Think about your journey of self-discovery. How do you differentiate between the narratives shaped by narcissistic figures and your authentic identity?

In your pursuit of closure, have you found ways to reclaim your sense of self and purpose, independent of validation or acknowledgment from others?

As you engage in therapeutic activities for healing, what emotions or insights arise during introspection and self-reflection?

MILESTONE GOALS

Readers need to gain a deeper understanding of the impact of narcissistic relationships on their sense of self and identity, allowing them to recognize and challenge distorted narratives perpetuated by toxic dynamics.

Readers need to cultivate self-compassion and acceptance as they navigate the complexities of forgiveness, prioritizing their emotional well-being and liberation from the expectations of societal norms. |107

- Readers need to engage in therapeutic activities and reflective exercises aimed at fostering healing and recovery from narcissistic abuse, empowering them to reclaim their narrative and embark on a journey of self-discovery and personal growth.

ACTIONABLE MOVEMENTS

1. **Self-Reflection Sessions:** Set aside dedicated time each week for self-reflection and introspection. Journal about your experiences, emotions, and insights gained from understanding the impact of narcissistic relationships on your life.

2. **Therapeutic Support:** Seek out therapy or counseling from professionals experienced in trauma and narcissistic abuse. Commit to regular sessions to explore and process your emotions, gain clarity, and develop coping strategies tailored to your needs.

3. **Narrative Rewriting:** Start rewriting your narrative by identifying and challenging distorted beliefs and narratives shaped by narcissistic relationships. Write down alternative, empowering narratives that reflect your authentic self and aspirations.

4. **Practice Self-Compassion:** Cultivate self-compassion by treating yourself with kindness, understanding, and patience. Challenge self-critical thoughts and replace them with affirmations and statements of self-acceptance and validation.

5. **Set Boundaries:** Establish clear boundaries in your relationships to protect your emotional well-being and assert your needs and preferences. Practice saying no when necessary and prioritize your needs without guilt or hesitation.

6. **Forgiveness Exploration:** Reflect on your attitudes towards forgiveness and explore what forgiveness means to you in the context of narcissistic relationships. Allow yourself to process feelings of anger, resentment, and hurt while considering the possibility of forgiveness as a personal choice rather than an obligation.

7. **Connect with Support Networks:** Contact supportive friends, family members, or online communities who understand and validate your experiences. Share your journey, seek advice, and support others navigating similar challenges.

8. **Set Realistic Expectations:** Recognize that healing from narcissistic abuse is gradual and nonlinear process. Set realistic expectations for your progress and celebrate small victories along the way.

9. **Celebrate Self-Discovery:** Embrace moments of self-discovery and personal growth as you navigate your healing journey. Acknowledge your strength, resilience, and progress towards living authentically and reclaiming your narrative.

In the empty pages ahead, you can explore this chapter more deeply and make it your own. Take this opportunity to write your thoughts, ideas, and questions about what you've read so far. Feel free to brainstorm, draw, or note down any questions that pop into your head.

Thank you!

We are constantly striving to provide the ideal experience for the community, and your input helps us to define that experience. So we kindly ask you when you have free time take a minute to post a review on Amazon.

Thank you for helping us support our passions.

Scan QR-CODE

and leave us a review on Amazon in just a few seconds

Made in the USA
Columbia, SC
15 October 2024

44391847R00063